Alex Taylor is an experienced youth worker and writer. He has been involved in youth work for almost 20 years in a variety of churches and settings. For twelve years, he worked for Scripture Union as an editor and creative developer. He has also written for Youth for Christ and Youthwork *Magazine, as well as Scripture Union. He leads Curtains Up, a performing arts-themed residential for 13- to 17-year-olds.*

Text copyright © Alex Taylor 2015
The author asserts the moral right
to be identified as the author of this work

Published by
The Bible Reading Fellowship
15 The Chambers, Vineyard
Abingdon OX14 3FE
United Kingdom
Tel: +44 (0)1865 319700
Email: enquiries@brf.org.uk
Website: www.brf.org.uk

BRF is a Registered Charity

ISBN 978 0 85746 248 0

First published 2015

10 9 8 7 6 5 4 3 2 1 0

Acknowledgements

Unless otherwise stated, scripture quotations are taken from The Holy Bible,
New International Version (Anglicised edition) copyright © 1979, 1984, 2011
by Biblica. Used by permission of Hodder & Stoughton Publishers, an Hachette
UK company. All rights reserved. 'NIV' is a registered trademark of Biblica. UK
trademark number 1448790.

Scripture quotations from the Good News Bible published by The Bible Societies/
HarperCollins Publishers Ltd, UK © American Bible Society 1966, 1971, 1976,
1992, used with permission.

Scripture quotations taken from the Holy Bible, New Living Translation, copyright
© 1996, 2004, 2007, 2013. Used by permission of Tyndale House Publishers, Inc.,
Carol Stream, Illinois 60188. All rights reserved.

Cover photo: Philip Lee Harvey/The Image Bank/Gettyimages

Every effort has been made to trace and contact copyright owners for material
used in this resource. We apologise for any inadvertent omissions or errors, and
would ask those concerned to contact us so that full acknowledgement can be
made in the future.

A catalogue record for this book is available from the British Library

Printed and bound by CPI Group (UK) Ltd, Croydon CR0 4YY

Reaching Young People

New ideas for your youth ministry

Edited by Alex Taylor

Contents

*Wayne Dixon describes a schools-based ministry
that has developed and grown over 20 years.*

*Andy Milne leads Sorted, a ministry among
young people in Bradford.*

*Jenni Creasy explores the interfaith ministry of The Feast,
which started in Birmingham but is now transferring to
other parts of the country.*

*Colin Stephenson and Tina Taylor tell the stories of Kerygma and
South Lakes Youth for Christ, and their bus ministries to
rural communities.*

*Tessa Oram has worked in education in Hull for many years, and
has seen much success with a low-key mentoring project.*

*James Henley explores how to reach out to the 16–30 age
group. How can we help older young people to remain part of a
worshipping community?*

*Kay Morgan-Gurr and Paula Smith consider how to welcome
young people with additional needs into our communities,
and look at the Wide Open residential.*

*Ricky Rew describes the ministry of Hope MK, a
project to help young people in Milton Keynes
make a difference to their community.*

*Amy Boucher relates the mission and ministry of ConfiDANCE,
a dance project that runs activities in churches,
schools and local communities.*

*How can young people be part of Messy Church communities?
Lucy Moore examines some of the issues.*

Introduction

The church has always wrestled with the well-being and nurture of young adults. In the past 100 years or so, that care has been expressed through concerns about unemployment, alcohol abuse and many other issues, leading Christians to set up programmes and clubs in order to help young adults out of difficult and damaging situations.

The 19th and early 20th centuries saw the birth of many organisations aimed at helping young people—the YMCA, football clubs (including Manchester City, Everton and Aston Villa) and the Scouting movement, to name but a few—all of them started by Christians with a heart to show the love of Jesus to young people.

However, teenagers as an age grouping started to be recognised only in the 1920s, and the word 'teenager' didn't come into common usage until the 1940s. In the decades since, churches have carried on working with and teaching young people in a variety of different ways.

Unfortunately, the number of young people in church in recent years has fallen dramatically. This is partly due to a fall in overall numbers, but young people in church have become proportionately more rare. Many young people now come from families whose most recent experience of church was two or even three generations ago.

Over the last 30 years or so, it seems that the church hasn't been able to keep pace with our constantly changing society. Or is it that we have clung too closely to the accepted ways of doing things in our particular church tradition? Then again, we may have fretted too much about the fact that the few numbers we have are shrinking further, while we ignore the many outside the church who have never heard about Christ.

We have to ask ourselves: is the current way that many of us in the church 'do' youth work working? It's a painful question to ask, but the statistics might suggest that we need to look afresh—completely afresh—at our thinking, methods and practices. Too many young people are missing out on hearing about Christ.

It's incredibly sad that so many young people have never heard the good news of Jesus, but it's also a great opportunity. We have the greatest story ever told, and we are not short of people to tell it to. How, then, should we go about it? Maybe you're in a church that has a long-established youth work, or maybe your congregation is only starting to think about reaching the young people in your community. Perhaps you're somewhere in between.

This book contains stories of people who have tried something new, something different, in order to reach out to young people from different backgrounds and in different situations. However, it is not simply a collection of inspiring stories. It's designed to help you think, 'That could happen in my town, in my parish, in my church,' and it's designed to give you help and advice on how to make a new ministry a reality.

Each church is different; each youth centre is different; each community is different. Your youth work is unique; no one knows your local context better than you. However, every so often, it's a good thing to take stock, to think about what you're doing and why. Who are you reaching out to? What could you do differently? What could you do that's new?

Sometimes we need to be brave. We might need to say, 'I don't think this is working; we need to stop and change.'

Alternatively, we may think, 'This is working really well; we should step things up and grow.' Many churches might find that some parts of their work are succeeding while other parts need refining.

Taking action

In order to reflect on how your current ministry is going, gather your youth work team together and list all the elements of your work. Assess how successful each part has been. Your assessment might revolve around the numbers of young people you attract, how successfully young people become part of your community or how much young people grow and move along in the spiritual journey. This final factor is most difficult to quantify. Many young people seem to take two steps forward and one step back (or maybe two or even five steps back), and what seems like growth in one week can all be 'undone' in the next.

Ask yourself this question too: am I expecting all my young people to fit in with one style of youth work? What suits one group of young people will not suit others, and it's likely that you'll have a mix of different interests, outlooks and personalities, even in a small group. How do we gauge success with that in mind?

However you measure success, it's likely that some elements of your ministry will be performing better than others. What are you going to do about that? You may decide to put more resources into the more successful areas, as these are where you're seeing growth in outreach or discipleship. Alternatively, you might pour more into areas that aren't yet succeeding, particularly if they are areas that God has specifically called you to. Just because something isn't working as you expected, it doesn't mean that God isn't part of the situation and that he won't bring it to fruition later on.

Of course, this objective way of viewing your work must be coupled with prayer—pouring your heart out to God about your passions, worries, hopes and dreams for the young people in your groups, and those you're reaching out to, and listening to what he says. Is he calling you to carry on, or to start something new?

None of the stories you're about to read is, in itself, the ultimate answer to your youth work needs. You will need to weigh up prayerfully how an idea might work for you and adapt some of the principles so that they will fit your situation. It is also important to consider these activities in the context of your wider church. How can you enthuse the leaders of your church community and the wider congregation? How can you get others involved practically and, more importantly, in prayer?

It's important not to choose an idea and dive headlong into it, tempting as that might be! We need to think through why we're going to set it up. How are we going to measure success? What is our methodology? Who is going to help oversee the work? How does it fit with other ministries in the area?

If a particular ministry doesn't fit your context, that's fine. Pray for the people involved—we are all on the same exciting journey—and move on to the next case study. But allow yourself to be challenged, and don't dismiss an idea straight away if its relevance to you isn't immediately obvious. Approach these inspiring stories in the presence of God and with an open mind, and let the Spirit run riot with your imagination.

It might be helpful to think about these principles as you go forward: be brave, work with others, be willing to fail, and hold your ministry lightly.

- **Be brave:** Don't be afraid to do things differently, or to stop something that's been going for a long time, or to try to reach a new set of young people, or to focus on one aspect of ministry and really go for it.
- **Work with others:** Get your own congregation to buy in to the ministry. Set aims and targets that the whole church signs up to. Try to partner with other churches to reach more. Don't be territorial: don't think of 'my young people' and 'your young people'. Everyone needs to hear the gospel message, and nothing gets in the way like being possessive.
- **Be willing to fail:** Sometimes things don't go well, and that's OK, as long as you learn from it. Don't start a ministry feeling apprehensive that it won't work: that will hold you back. Agree aims and targets before you start, and make sure that your church leadership is part of this process. This will help you to measure how well you do, and it means that everyone will take responsibility for the work.
- **Hold your ministry lightly:** Invest in the work, get passionate, and love your young people. But remember, it's not your ministry, it's God's. If you need to make changes, holding it lightly means you won't cling on to something long after it's become obsolete. And if God calls you to move on from your church community, the ministry won't collapse when you leave.

1

HAM: Hanging around ministry

Wayne Dixon is a schools worker for Christian Connections in Schools, a schools-work trust working in Slough, Windsor and Maidenhead. For over 25 years, Wayne has been going into schools, developing relationships with students and staff alike. During that time, he has developed a ministry that he calls 'HAM: Hanging Around Ministry', which has met with great success and some not inconsiderable challenges.

Why HAM?

In my early days as a schools worker, my approach was 'assembly and a lunchtime follow-up session'. My reasoning was this: if anyone was interested in what I said during the assembly and wanted to chat further, I would be available during the lunchtime session. In a small way, it worked, but it depended on students being keen and remembering to come.

One day, I did my assembly, then, at lunchtime, I waited and waited and waited in the appointed room. No one came. This wasn't a problem: we should expect lean times as well as times of great harvest, after all. However, towards the end of lunch, a lad came in and we chatted. At the end he said, 'Oh, by the way, Wayne, some of my friends wanted to come, but were too embarrassed.'

How, then, could I be more open to approach by the young people? Obviously, the method of getting the young people to come to where I was, on my terms, was putting some students off. Perhaps they didn't want to be seen doing 'holy stuff', or didn't want to ask big questions in front of their friends.

From then on, my approach changed. I decided simply to be 'around'. I wasn't going to announce it to the students; I would just be there. This decision was greatly influenced by the day I spent with Kenny Wilson, a schools worker who, at that time, was based in a school in Oxford. Because he had a base in the school and existing relationships, he was able to be present in a way that I, as a worker who visited different schools, couldn't be at that time. Spending time with Kenny enabled me to observe how 'hanging around' worked. His relationship with the young people was more informal: they had a rapport that I warmed to.

There is still a place for the organised and formal approach —for example, running an assembly, RE lesson or starting a new Christian group—but these times work hand-in-hand with the unannounced and informal. There is an element of risk and fear in starting this kind of ministry, as students (and staff, even though you will have got their permission in advance) initially wonder what you're doing there, but these difficulties soon pale as you start to form good relationships and have some great conversations.

For me, HAM is about 'being there'. When you're doing an assembly, lesson or Christian group, it's specific and focused: you have a reason to be there, and you're expected to be there. My observations are that young people like to talk and they appreciate you giving the time to be there, but you can't really get to know people in an assembly. However, the assembly gives you a platform on which to be seen, and a link is then created when you hang around afterwards. Students look forward to it—just as I miss it when it doesn't happen—and sometimes they've said, 'We haven't seen you for a while!'

Then, when they want to talk about God (and sometimes they do), you can meet that need. Your conversations can reinforce what you've done in assembly, but they also give you the time to get to know people better. Sometimes HAM has led to a request from staff to get alongside a particular student to listen, chat and just be a link for them if there is a concern, difficulty or problem. If school, parents and the student are happy, this too can make a difference to an individual.

Why even bother with schools work?

This is a very fair question and worth asking from time to time. My suggested answer would be: we bother going into school because it's where most children and young people are. Here are some useful statistics and facts:

- In 1904, 56 per cent of children and young people went to church. Today that figure has dropped to only four per cent.
- 39 per cent of churches have no one under the age of 11.
- 49 per cent of churches have no one between the ages of 11 and 14.
- 59 per cent of churches have no one between the ages of 15 and 19.
- 99 per cent of children and young people are in school.
- 80 per cent of those who become Christians do so before the age of 18.

Of course, we should not forget the four per cent of our children and young people who are in our churches, as they play a crucial role in our schools. It seems to me that part of our role in churches is to equip and encourage, enthuse and enable, motivate and move such young people to share Jesus appropriately where they spend most of their time—in school.

A typical HAM session

Before the day begins, I have a plan of where in the school I'm going to go, and when. Having signed in, I start in the common room before lunch, as students are usually in there. This is the territory of Years 12 and 13, and we chat about anything and everything. When the lunch bell rings, I leave the common room, as it gets packed, and move into the next part of my routine. I might start with lunch, where I'll sit with some students and chat while we eat.

Then I'll go on a walkabout around the outdoor communal areas of the school. There are often some specific groups to meet up with, which is great, as this gives the opportunity to maintain relationships with young people. There are also some unusual and unplanned encounters. Some students approach me, wanting to chat through the good and bad of life, and these are amazing opportunities of sharing, myth-busting and relationship-building.

When the bell rings, I might pop into a class registration (if I have that kind of relationship with the teacher), or I might head back to the common room or staff room, and that's it till the next time. It's not complex and there's no secret formula to follow. It's a matter of making myself available to talk to the members of the school community in the most appropriate ways possible.

Being in school, hanging around with members of the community, opens the door to taking part in other elements of school life—events such as school productions, music concerts, sports days, speech days and the like. These events are key parts of the life of the school and are the times when students form lasting memories of their time there.

The common room

The common room is possibly the most relaxing place to be in a school. It's the place to be for chat, music, games, study, birthday cake and much more. Of course, we need to exercise wisdom and sensitivity: recently I looked into a common room and made a quick about turn as I heard a member of staff begin to let rip at the students. I got the signal that this was not an appropriate time for 'hanging around'!

If I arrive in school around lunchtime, I pop in before the bell rings and catch up with whoever is around. When the room starts to fill up, as I've mentioned, I go elsewhere and connect with other areas of the school. At the end of lunch, I may revisit the common room. It's also a good place to be just after an assembly, especially if Years 12 and 13 have been in the assembly. The best times are when the discussion focuses on Jesus. Because the students are on their own territory, they are often relaxed enough to chat, discuss and debate the issues.

I don't have the Bible hidden behind my back and my opening sentence is not, 'Have you been washed in the blood of the Lamb?' As you might imagine, that wouldn't be well received. It's important to give space for people to explore the questions they want to ask, and good relationships are a key to that. Once, I went to the common room after delivering a lesson. It was break time, so the room was packed, but at the end of break and for the next hour a few students and I chewed the fat on a whole range of subjects. I came away thinking, 'That's what it's all about!' The common room is a place where people can really get to grips with all of life's issues, and those times are among the highlights of being in school—unpredictable, unplanned, but significant.

The staff room

I love staff rooms now, but this has not always been the case. When I started as a schools worker, I had a great fear of the staff room. Not being a teacher myself, I felt it was alien territory, so I often stayed away. However, it's important to form good relationships with the staff, as this creates greater openness and trust. The better they know you, the happier they are to allow you to work in their school. If I'm in school at break time, teachers might say, 'Come to the staff room for a coffee', and I decline because I'd prefer to be out with the young people, but I often go to the staff room before school or assembly, before and after break, and before and after lunch.

I turned up once to a school for some HAM, went into the staff room and was greeted by staff in unusual attire. It was an INSET day, so there were no pupils around, but it was lunchtime so I stayed and had the most amazing chat with some of the staff. Often, I've chatted with staff for a long time about a wide range of topics. Again, there's a need for genuine wisdom and sensitivity, as they are working, and such relationships take time to develop, but chatting to teachers in this way is the most fantastic privilege.

Tragedies in school

What can you say when words are not enough? The toughest aspect of being a schools worker, for me, has been facing the times when tragedy has struck a school community. I don't think you can ever be prepared for the experience. When it comes, it's rough and tough. Once I was asked by a mother to speak at the funeral of her daughter, who had died after a long illness. Such funerals, where tears stream as hundreds mourn the loss of a friend, often lead to the question 'Why did God allow this?' There is no real, genuine or satisfying answer: the 'why' remains.

What I have learned in these extreme occasions is to be silent, just to be there, and, if appropriate, to offer some words of comfort.

Prayer

One of the soundbites I use most regularly is 'Prayer is the *most* significant contribution we can make to our schools.' When parents have initiated prayer groups for schools, usually for a short season, it has been superb.

I met Doris a few years ago at the Langley Free Church women's meeting. What a lovely lady she was. She lived opposite Langley Grammar School and said, 'Before, I saw schools as a bit of a nuisance. Now I see them as a topic for prayer.' And that's how she used them for many years. Sadly she is no longer with us, but there are many people like Doris in our churches, who have a real heart and prayer ministry for our schools, and I'm very grateful for them.

Church connections

Very rarely do young people or staff come up to me in school and say, 'I'd really like to go along to church,' but if they do, I encourage a young person to attend somewhere local ideally, and, if possible, with peers or friends they know. Many years ago, two teenagers with no church background went on a Scripture Union holiday, and I was contacted to see if I could suggest a local church for them. I made contact with them in their school and encouraged them to go to a local church. They decided not to attend, but at least the mechanism was there, to put them in touch. I have sometimes invited people I know to my own church. Most say 'no', which is discouraging, but others say 'yes'. Church is important, but should not be made into a stumbling-block or the be-all and end-all. The challenge is to try to make the bridge shorter without changing or compromising the message.

As I've already said, HAM is about 'being there'. Young people really appreciate the chance to talk to adults who are not outright authority figures in their lives (as teachers or their parents are). Honest and open relationships with schools, staff and students can lead to great opportunities to show love and share faith.

'Hanging around' in your own context

- Be you, yourself and no one else.
- Make sure the head teacher or a member of senior staff is happy for you to hang around. (At the main school where I do this, the head is retiring soon, and I have no idea if the new head will be happy for me to continue. Until I get that permission, I won't be able to do HAM there.)
- Always sign in and observe the school protocols.
- Be aware that, initially, you may feel vulnerable. People may wonder why you are there or resent your presence on their territory.
- Don't take the school for granted. Always remember that you are a guest there.
- Watch where you go. For example, if I enter a common room and there's only one student there, I don't stay.

- Listen and talk. If I'm chatting with a group and they are talking about football, I'm on familiar ground and we can have a good discussion. If I'm with a group and the subject is skateboarding or computer games, I have no idea, so I listen and learn. On one occasion, I took an observer into school. We were with a group who were chatting about a band I had never heard of. However, my observer knew the band and was able to have a great conversation. All I could do was listen and learn.

I believe there is enormous value and potential in HAM for a variety of different people, not just schools workers, youth workers or church leaders. I do not underestimate the difficulties, particularly when starting out. As I've said, initially you will feel outside your comfort zone, but if you already have a relationship with a school, this lends itself to developing HAM if it is appropriate for you. It is not everyone's cup of tea, but, whatever our involvement with schools—formal, informal or a bit of both—it is very worthwhile.

2
Sorted

Andy Milne runs Sorted, a fresh expressions project working with young people in Bradford. Based in schools but also reaching out to groups such as skaters, Sorted now reaches over 100 young people, many of whom have never before belonged to a church community. Sorted is a Church Army project backed by Church Army funding.

Training

In late 2003, my wife Tracy and I moved back to our home town of Bradford with a sense that God was calling us to start a youth church. Having been away training at Wilson Carlile College of Evangelism in Sheffield for a few years, we returned with the belief that we needed to start this new youth community through relationship-building and by empowering young people. I hoped to do this through detached youth work, small groups and eventually a youth congregation. It was exciting and scary: I had lots of ideas but didn't really know if any of them would work.

One of the first things we did was to gather a team of volunteers from local churches. We met weekly to chat over coffee, pray together and discuss our vision and values through a series of training sessions. We lost some volunteers during this process, but gained others. As time went along, it was great to see a community forming of people who were growing in friendship and growing as a team.

We initially planned to train together for six to ten weeks but ended up extending the training period to nearly six months. Why? It simply didn't seem right to stop. Six months might sound excessively long but by the end of it we weren't just a team; we had become a community—a good environment to bring young people into as we grew closer as a Christian family. We would reap the benefits of the six months' training period in the years to come. We started with a stable team who stuck together despite some big challenges.

Starting out

During my first year, we started meeting up with young people by playing football and doing skateboarding in the area where we lived. Despite seeing a couple of young people come to faith, we simply weren't going to meet enough young people this way to start a youth church. After the team training was complete, the volunteers started doing detached youth work in pairs. Although this gave them an insight into the culture of local young people, most of the volunteers simply weren't cut out to be detached workers, so this approach wasn't very fruitful. A third attempt at mission happened as I started co-leading a lunch club in Immanuel College. We played games and did short talks, but it was hard to build deep relationships through this once-a-week club. As I prayed, I sensed that I needed to be in the school more often, but in a different role.

In 2004, I started doing detached youth work on the playground of Immanuel. Over the next couple of years, I got to know loads of young people. Going into school simply to listen and get alongside young people, my encounters were initially limited to one big group of skaters and their mates, as they were the most open to having me around. It took longer for other groups to accept me but, over time, contacts were made, which led to the building of trust and of friendships. I still know many of these young people today.

In April 2005, we started our open youth session on Friday nights and simply invited young people from the playground and the neighbourhood. By the end of the summer, we had about 30 young people meeting to skateboard, play football, chat and listen to music.

We would do a short talk or discussion about God or a life

issue halfway through the session. The young people had no church connection, so we were talking about God to a crowd that seemed uninterested and rowdy. One or two came to faith, but it was a big achievement just to get the group to listen for five minutes each week. We kept asking: how could we get lots of these people connecting with God and change the crowd into a Christian community?

Focusing on what mattered

We stumbled on the answer to this question as we kept focusing on being relational. Over the next year, many of the youngsters from the Friday night crowd would meet with Tracy and me or another couple during the week in small groups.

Some little groups prayed and read the Bible because they included a key person who was open to doing so. Others just chatted, and we prayed for opportunities to share our faith as we opened up our home. As the next year rolled on, relationships deepened and quite a few young people started a journey of faith. The community of adults that had met in 2004 was expanding and starting to become a community with the young people.

Late in 2006, we sensed that God wanted us to start a worship service. How could we do this and stay true to our values of being both relational and giving young people ownership? We decided to ask key members of the small groups to join with us in starting a worship service. We planned everything in detail with them because we wanted them to own it, so the conversation went like this: I said we needed a worship time; they said we needed a break in the middle of the service. I said we needed teaching from the

Bible; they said it had to be fun and interactive. Together we worked it out, and we were challenged to listen to them and affirm their contributions.

As the service got going, we found that the most important part of it was experiential. We experimented with different ways of praying, but it was difficult to get young people with short attention spans to be still and quiet as we waited in God's presence, so we hit upon a way of praying that really worked with them. We would pray and ask God to come by his Holy Spirit. We would then lay hands on two or three key young people before releasing them to go and do the same for their peers (while we followed just behind). We found that people with short concentration spans were staying focused because they were participating and taking an active part in the process.

Without ever planning it this way, we began to see that Sorted comprised four stages of a spiritual journey:

1 Schools work where relationships started.
2 An open activity session on Friday nights for young people to discover Sorted and hear a short message about God.
3 Small groups where they could ask questions and discuss faith, starting to become disciples.
4 A youth worship service where they could encounter God and go deeper with him.

All four stages became crucial to the ministry's success. Young people with little or no previous church connection find it easier to progress through a set of stages than to jump straight in at stage 4: an act of worship, such as a service, can seem alien at first. We also found that relationships, ownership and faith in God often deepen as young people move on to another stage. This is partly because we meet them more often, but also because each stage has a distinct purpose that builds on the previous stage.

Seeds of faith get planted in both the schools work and the open activity session, but young people often find God and become Christians in the small groups and worship service. You might ask, then, why bother with the schools work and open session if the small groups and worship services are where young people find God? The answer is that relationships and trust need building in stages 1 and 2 so that the deeper teaching, prayer and worship will happen in a safe environment where young people feel unpressured and are able to discover God at a pace they are happy with.

If young people drop out of the worship service for a while, it's easy for them to come back because they are still part of Sorted on other nights. They already have a sense of belonging by the time they find God in stages 3 or 4, which means that they are more likely to stay in Sorted and be nurtured in their newfound faith.

Meet Carl

In April 2005, I was telling young people in Immanuel College about the new Friday night open session we had just started. A 13-year-old lad called Carl started chatting to me. He asked me why I was in school, so I told him about the idea for Sorted and he came along to the session.

Carl and I got on well; he quickly became interested in God and became a Christian. After a while, though, he drifted off, met a group of Satanists and got into Satanism. At first we argued a lot about it, until someone wisely advised me to keep a harmonious relationship with Carl so that the door would remain open for him to return to God.

After a few weeks, Carl confessed to me that Satanism was messing his head up, so I offered to pray with him. What followed was something like deliverance, as Carl described an experience of being released and then feeling God's power flow into his life. He opened his eyes and said, 'Wow, when you prayed it felt as if something came out of me and then something better came into me.' Awesome!

You would expect the story to get better but, sadly, it didn't. Carl started attending both a small group and the worship service but gradually became more out of line over the next couple of years. I ended up having to ban him a couple of times, but he still continued to disrupt things. Eventually, we decided to ban Carl for a couple of months because he constantly upset both our plans and others in the group.

When Carl returned to Sorted, I was nervous, expecting more trouble, but I didn't need to be. Carl soon came back to God and wanted to get involved in helping us run Sorted. We took it slowly at first, but, as he moved into his late teens, Carl grew into leadership. He's happy to serve and is a good spokesman for God at the front or in a small group. Carl has organised events on Friday nights and is a key player within Sorted. His faith has flourished in the last few years— so much so that he now works for Sorted as a full-time Christian youth worker.

Carl's story taught me a huge lesson: we should never give up on anyone, because we don't know how they might change, especially when God is involved. There are times when I've been tempted to give up on a young person who constantly disrupts, yet Carl's story reminds me to persevere.

Relationship and ownership

Before moving back to Bradford, we had read Luke 10 and felt inspired to go to the places where young people hang out so that we could build relationships with them in those places. We hoped that this would enable us to find 'people of peace' and then form small groups. Detached work in the school playground became the most fruitful way for this to happen.

As the relationships formed, I would see if there were one or two key young people who were especially open to me or the gospel, get to know them and then try to start a small group with them and their mates. As we started meeting weekly with the new small group, we gained an understanding about their culture (including local culture and teen tribe subculture and worldview) and could work with the key youngsters to organise group discussions about God or life issues that were relevant to the group.

As the group grew, so did the members' Christian faith and our own understanding of their culture, all fostered through the developing relationships. For example, we would use life stories from skateboarding culture and get young people to make crosses out of skateboards when working with skaters. With football-mad young people, we'd use discussion questions such as 'Is God the referee, the team captain, the crowd member or the best player?'

Our small group meetings included around 20 minutes for discussion and an hour to do whatever activities the young people like. One group called it 'chill and chat'. They said I should choose the topic to chat about and they would choose the activity for the chill time each week. This arrangement guaranteed their ownership as they got to make key decisions about what the group would do. As we hung out to skateboard or play basketball informally, young people would often share issues with me out of earshot of their peers.

It was from these small beginnings—by staying focused on building relationships, faith and ownership—that our Christian community formed. However, as the numbers of young people became much larger in the following years, we had to work much harder to keep growing relationships, faith and ownership in bigger groups.

The growth of these larger groups led to periods when the young people would lapse into 'consumer' mode, with the adults running around, providing for them, while they only took what they wanted. We were often left with the rubbish and the cigarette ends to clear up. As we struggled to work out what to do, our key young people seemed rooted to the sidelines, powerless to get involved and feeling that things were becoming very unSorted!

We discovered that, to counter this consumerist mentality, each large session (between 15 and 60 members) always needed to be co-led by a team of young people. Tracy and I picked up these young people in the car and set up the equipment with them—table tennis and skate ramps for the activity session, Bibles and chairs for the small groups, or PA and microphones for the worship service. We gave them all roles and listened to their input. This changed the atmosphere, as influence swung back to the key young people. After a while, most of the people attending the groups wanted to help out by being part of the team.

Meet Josh

During my first year in Immanuel College, I got to know a group of skaters and moshers through doing detached youth work in the school playground. I spent a lot of time hanging out with one particular group, the youngest member of which was Josh. One day, I sensed the Holy Spirit saying that Josh was a 'person of peace' (Luke 10:6) and would be a key member of the group. Not quite sure what this meant, I decided to do my best simply to get to know Josh and then see what would happen.

A few weeks later, I suggested to the skaters that we meet up after school, go skateboarding and become a group. Most of them turned up and we had a good skate, but, from the second week onwards, the only person to come was Josh. He was quiet yet friendly, shy yet engaging, already a Christian, and had many friends who were not yet Christians. Together with an adult volunteer, I met with Josh every Wednesday to skate and chat. We were sometimes joined by one or two other friends, but often it was just Josh.

Nine months later, Josh really came into his own as a 'person of peace'. Being unable to get his friends out on Wednesdays, we tried to set up another group on Tuesday nights, so that his friends could make it. This group became very fruitful as several young people became Christians over time. Josh became a bridge between his mates and me, inviting most of them to the group. We met each Tuesday night to pray, discuss a Bible passage and then simply have fun. It was this group that devised the 'chill and chat' format mentioned above. Shortly afterwards, the Wednesday afternoon group took off as well.

Josh is a good example of someone who already believed in God and whom God used to help us make connections with his mates. The fact that he was well respected among his peers, coupled with his openness to God, enabled us to reach out to his mates through him.

Over the next few years, Josh's leadership skills developed as he calmly bridged the gap between skaters and other youth tribes, leading a small group within Sorted. Despite being a skater, he was able to lead a group of people from a different 'tribe' with totally different interests, and gained huge respect from them.

Looking to the future

Meet Matty

Matty started coming to Sorted with Carl and we soon got to know him and his brother. Matty became enthusiastic about God and was keen to get involved. When our youth worship service began, he was an obvious person to invite. Within a few weeks, Tracy and Matty started leading a monthly teaching slot together. Tracy's experience and knowledge, coupled with Matty's willingness to learn and speak in front of his peers, worked well.

By 2007, Matty had preached on his own without Tracy. It was a great encouragement to hear him speak passionately about God. The young people listened keenly with an interest that often wasn't present when an adult spoke.

Matty then stopped coming to Sorted. He had a new group of friends and went off with them, doing what they did. This all seemed to happen very quickly, within the space of a month. Despite having good intentions to return, he dropped out of Sorted for several years. This was hard for Tracy and me to take. We were really sad when he stopped coming, as we were about a few other young people who'd left after we'd grown close to them, spent a lot of time with them and invested a lot of hope in them. It made us question what God was doing and whether we were getting things wrong.

However, becoming a father changed Matty's life dramatically. Since then, he has matured a lot. Over the past year, he has been involved in a group we've set up for young parents and is currently exploring ways of using the skills he learnt with Tracy to help with the running of a parenting group.

When we started Sorted with young people like Matty, we wondered what would happen when they hit the age of 18. Many of them have little or no experience of church and are unlikely to start attending a traditional church when they reach adulthood. As our first young people reached 16 and 17, they started asking the question: would Sorted still be available for them when they turned 18? As we prayed, we sensed that our calling was to plant a church so that young people would become the leaders of Sorted and take it into adulthood.

Matty is one of several young people who stopped coming to Sorted at some point but either came back or came into contact with us again as a young adult. We are currently working out how we can best do church for and with young adults. 'Thrive' is the name of the parenting group that has started with this purpose in mind, because many people in North Bradford become parents between the ages of 18 and 22. We're also exploring ways to engage with young adults in pubs and other places where they naturally hang out.

Sorted continues to grow, moving beyond the community that started at Immanuel College. In 2009, following a time of discernment, we started another youth church, Sorted 2, which grew out of a secondary school called Hanson Academy, one of the largest schools in the UK. This was a scary step of faith: we strongly felt God calling us to go for it, even though we didn't know where all the resources were going to come from. In time, God provided through Church

Army UK and local churches. Sorted 2 has now developed into a youth church with many young people involved.

Some of the young adults who are now too old to be considered 'young people' in the Sorted community are helping to start a Sorted 3 for younger teens from Immanuel College. Sorted 1, 2 and 3 operate as three distinct communities, despite the overlap of leadership. Each meets as a community between one and three times a week, but some young people from each Sorted come together for summer camps and one-off events.

Urban outreach in your own context

If you are interested in using some of the methods and values mentioned in this chapter, here are a few pointers to get you started:

- Pray and listen to God with others. God can open doors and make things happen.
- Find good partners. Local churches have prayed with us and supported us with finance for resources, use of their premises and volunteers.
- Develop your team. We started both Sorted 1 and Sorted 2 with a team made up of eight to twelve adults, mainly from local churches. We spent several months meeting weekly to worship, pray, plan and do training sessions based on key values such as discernment, relationship-building with young people, empowering young people, running small groups and teamwork.
- Start building relationships with young people in your local secondary school. Detached work is ideal, but, if this option isn't available, you could run a lunch club, offer

to read to or mentor young people or support the school in any way that enables you to build relationships with young people. Your involvement might start small, but, as you get known and trusted in the school, it is likely to lead to more or better opportunities to build relationships. Also, look for ways to build relationships with young people in your local area, perhaps through detached youth work.

- Look for young 'people of peace'—those who are open to you and/or the gospel. Build relationships with those young people, form little groups with them and start exploring the Christian faith.
- Start an open youth session with the aim of enabling lots of young people to join you and bring their friends. We always ask, 'What do you want to do?' so that young people can choose their own activities. Perhaps the next question should be, 'How can you make it happen?' so that they start taking ownership of organising the activities with your support.
- Start a youth worship service with your key young people. Involve them in developing teaching, worship and prayer that are both relevant and appropriate for your context. We've always found that creating spaces where young people can encounter God is key. This might mean praying with them to encounter God at some point in the service.
- Keep asking yourself: is what we're doing bringing more young people to Jesus and making disciples? Is what we're doing deepening relationships and increasing ownership so that Christian community or church is being created? If yes, then great. If no, then prayerfully reflect and consider what needs to change.

3

The Feast

*The Feast is a schools
work trust that began
as an associate trust to
Scripture Union. It started
in Birmingham but is now
setting up similar ministries
in other areas of the country.
It seeks to bring young
people of different faiths
together in order to encourage
dialogue, understanding
and friendships. The hope
is that this continuing work
will break down some of the
barriers between the different
communities in Birmingham
and other cities in which
The Feast is starting to work.
Jenni Creasy, a schools
worker for The Feast in
Birmingham, tells the story of
this groundbreaking ministry.*

The need for dialogue

Britain is a multicultural country, and nowhere is this more obvious than in our large towns and cities. However, despite the mixture of backgrounds and nationalities, communities tend to be segregated, especially by ethnicity and faith. This is certainly true of Britain's second-largest city, Birmingham. Here we find large pockets of Pakistani, Bangladeshi, Somali, Caribbean, white and other communities living closely, yet very separately. It's difficult for young people to mix with peers from other backgrounds when communities are separate and often suspicious of each other. Dialogue between different groups is scarce, not only due to a lack of opportunities to meet but also because of a lack of skills in expressing opinions and accepting differences.

Dr Andrew Smith (also known as Smeeee) was a schools worker with Scripture Union in Birmingham, spending a lot of time in schools where the majority of pupils were Muslim. He became increasingly frustrated by the ease with which discussions about faith would dissolve into arguments. Many young people weren't able to listen and be understanding when talking about faith; rather, they resorted to shouting and insisting that they were right.

Andrew was also attending interfaith events for adults, which were, more often than not, dull affairs. He began to wonder if interfaith events aimed at young people would help to prevent the cycle of arguments. He knew that the activities would need to be more interesting and diverse than the adult versions he attended, but he was convinced that they would go a long way to breaking down barriers between communities.

He started to run 'Youth Encounter' events, which saw

large groups of Muslim, Christian and Sikh teenagers gather to take part in different activities. He ran one or two a year, and then started to organise residentials for smaller groups of boys. After running one of these smaller events, he realised that better conversations happened where there were fewer numbers and only two faiths involved, and was keen to see more of them develop.

With the help of Scripture Union, Andrew began the process of forming a trust to develop the work further. In partnership with the local community, he recruited trustees and raised funds to employ the first schools worker. In September 2009, Natasha Griffiths started working for the newly formed Feast Schools Work Trust.

By September 2010, the work had grown to such an extent that The Feast employed a project manager, Tim Fawssett, and a second schools worker, Jennifer Creasy. Thanks to this increased capacity, The Feast was able to run more events, work in more schools and expand the activities by attracting new churches and mosques to get involved.

In 2010, we employed our first Muslim youth worker, Nahim Khan. Soon afterwards we changed from charity status to a business with charitable status, to give our trustees more protection as we became national, and to make it easier for us to trade in the future. In April 2013, an administrator joined our team, followed by a youth worker for Bradford and Keighley in Yorkshire. We've seen steady growth in our short time of operating, and expect to see more.

What The Feast does

Our aim is to bring young people of different faiths together to talk about their beliefs in a safe and peaceful environment.

It's all about providing a space for young people who wouldn't normally meet each other to hang out, have fun and make friends with someone from a different faith. So far, The Feast has helped hundreds of young people from Muslim, Christian, Sikh and Hindu backgrounds to get together to explore their faiths, make new friends and have their lives changed by these encounters.

We usually have about twelve young people at each event, as we've found that keeping it small helps young people to mix and make friends more easily. There is less of a temptation to stick with the friends they came with. Once we have them all together in the same room, we simply run sessions that are exciting, energetic and relevant to them. It is essential to spend a good amount of time at the beginning to break the ice and get the young people talking, so we ensure that this element is never rushed.

Once the young people feel at ease with each other, we introduce the 'Guidelines for Dialogue' and we all agree to stick to them, so that everyone feels free and comfortable to talk about what they believe (see www.thefeast.org.uk/resources/guidelines-for-dialogue/). The young people then participate in lively discussions on a variety of different topics linked to their day-to-day life, finding out what the others think and believe. The discussion is driven by the young people; adult leaders are there to help, but they are encouraged to keep quiet and allow the young people to speak, even if they get it 'wrong'. This helps young people to grow in confidence to articulate their faith, rather than relying on adults around them. They are free to say, 'I don't know' and even opt out of the discussion completely if they feel uncomfortable. We've found that, most of the time, young people enjoy talking about their beliefs and opinions.

They are happy to admit when they're not sure and are accepted by others when they do so.

These youth events are often based on a theme or a chance to learn a new skill. We've used drama, sport, magic workshops, poetry, breakdancing and even comedy to bring different people together. Those attending the event find that they can enjoy doing things with new people and have much in common. It builds their confidence in both faith articulation and in practical skills, so it is really worthwhile.

Several times a year, we run weekends away for young people, from a Friday evening until Sunday afternoon. These are always single-sex events, as some communities have concerns about boys and girls mixing, especially when they're away overnight together. It's always been easier to run boys' residentials; however, we've done several girls' weekends away too. The events usually take place at an outdoor centre so that we can combine dialogue and outdoor education. We take groups of about ten young people, who are often meeting each other for the first time at the start of the trip. We mix them up right from the start, with one Muslim and one Christian sharing each room. Lots of games and team-building activities are included at the start to help build an atmosphere of trust. Dialogue sessions are incorporated throughout the weekend and are usually based on a theme, such as 'being a young man/woman of God'. Some of the best conversations happen in informal times, such as around the campfire. These weekends are really exciting, as the young people often get to know each other much better than they do at afternoon events. It is great to watch close friendships developing over such a short space of time.

In addition to the dialogue events, we help to engage young people in social action. This is a positive result of the good friendships that are formed through events. We find that, when barriers are overcome, young people strive to make their neighbourhoods and the wider world around them a better place. We've encouraged them to volunteer with local charities, such as Foodbank, to take part in litter picks and also to campaign about political issues.

This is a natural response and progression for the young people: once they have realised that the 'other' isn't as bad as they initially anticipated, they also find they are passionate about similar issues affecting the world around them. Together they find ways to help make a difference in their communities and become visible peacemakers to their neighbours.

Work in schools

Schools are essential to the work we currently do, and, in many instances, schools work is the way we attract young people to our events. We've worked in nine secondary schools across Birmingham since starting in 2009, organising clubs that help students to engage in interfaith and social action issues as well as to develop skills as young leaders. We also take assemblies, run enrichment day workshops and organise interfaith walks. The work varies, depending on the schools' needs and requirements: we get a lot of requests to come in and help meet their community cohesion aims and to assist their students in learning to talk about faith.

The schools where we work are predominantly Muslim-majority schools. One of the main reasons for this is that Christian young people tend to go to youth clubs or groups run by their churches, even though they might go to a variety of different secondary schools. Through their church, they meet other Christian young people who don't go to their school. This is not the same for Muslim young people. They may attend madrassah (or mosque school, where Muslim children learn to read the Qu'ran and pray), but this set-up is very different from a youth group, and many stop attending in their early teens. In our early days of facilitation, we found that it was easier to work with a Muslim-majority school than to go through the mosques. We have since worked with more mixed schools, as well as predominantly secular ones, and we have worked more closely with mosques.

Akaash's story

Akaash is a young Muslim from Birmingham. He goes to a school where almost all of the pupils are south-Asian Muslim, like himself. He got involved with The Feast through his school and has loved the opportunity to meet different people and learn about their faith. He thought that Christians would be really racist before he became involved with The Feast, but found them to be likeable people with whom he had things in common. 'The impact it's had on me, and how it's changed the way I think about other people, would be good for other people to experience too,' he says.

For Akaash, it's had a huge impact on the way he perceives Christians and has helped him to understand much more of what they think and believe. As a result, he now views the faith much more positively.

Work with religious communities

Religious communities are another key part of our work and we invest a lot of time in developing good relationships with mosques, churches and youth groups. Knowing the needs, concerns and leaders of religious groups enables us to work out how best to get them involved and help them in their interfaith relations. We often visit church youth groups before an event to run a Bible study with them, helping them to see why and how they should share their faith with peers from other religions. This helps to reduce any fears they might have about attending an event, and helps us get to know them before we introduce them to a group of Muslim young people.

Many churches across the city support our work. Whenever a church expresses interest, we put on special 'prayer and curry' nights. These are aimed at adults but we always invite young people to share their experiences with the congregation. They generate prayer and financial support and help us to build trust with the wider church community. We organised a pizza night in a mosque once, with a similar set-up, and it's possible that we will do this more often in the future.

The Istanbul Exchange

The Istanbul Exchange was an exciting development in 2011 and 2012 that took our work overseas. We worked alongside World Vision Lebanon to bring together young people from the West Midlands and Beirut to spend time exploring their faith and making friends. We met in Turkey, as it was neutral territory and easy for both parties to access. The event opened up new challenges involved in crossing many different cultures, as well as mixing up different denominations within both Islamic and Christian traditions.

Both trips involved 16 young people, some of whom had never left their own country. Spending a whole week together allowed us time to build up trusting relationships and explore topics that were normally taboo, especially for our Lebanese participants. Religion and politics are usually no-go areas for them, yet we found that we were able to have fruitful and peaceful discussions, sticking to the Guidelines for Dialogue. Both these weeks in 2011 and 2012 had a profound effect on everyone who took part, and helped us to see how The Feast's methods could be used in other cultures.

Sarah's story

Young people who have been involved in this ministry have seen huge benefits. One girl, Sarah, who came from a small town outside Birmingham, developed great confidence in befriending Muslims, even though she didn't encounter them in her day-to-day life. She went along to lots of events, including the Istanbul Exchange in 2011. This helped her to learn how to befriend Muslims and tell them what she believed. When she started university, she became close friends with a Muslim student, whom she then lived with for her second year of study. 'I don't think the relationship would have been so close if I hadn't learnt what I did with The Feast,' she comments.

Sarah is able to talk about what she believes with her Muslim friend and remains very close to her, even when they disagree. This is the kind of impact we want to have on young people, equipping them to have meaningful, honest and close relationships with believers from other faiths and to share their own faith well. Sarah was able to learn these skills while she was young, which has been of benefit to her in her adult life. She knows how to share the hope within her with gentleness and respect.

Impact on young people

The stereotypes and biases in young people's minds are due largely to the environment they've grown up in, so, when their attitudes are transformed by attending Feast events, this sometimes leads them, in turn, to challenge the prejudices and misconception in their families and religious communities. When they realise that it's possible to be friends with people even when they disagree on something as important as faith, they see that there is potential for a more integrated future. This may go against their parents' experience and comes as a surprise.

A fine example is the story of two young men from a very right-wing area of Birmingham who went to one of the lads' weekends away and had an amazing time mixing with other young people, both Christians and Muslims. They came back and did a presentation in their church, emphasising the personal connections and new friendships they'd made. They said, 'I thought I was going to share a room with a Muslim, but I shared with Ali, who's now my friend.'

Their presentation deeply challenged members of the church, and one woman decided that she needed to make more effort in talking to people from other faiths. She acted on her decision the very next day, speaking to a Muslim woman she'd seen every day at work but had never engaged in conversation. It's fantastic to see how young people can have such an impact on adults in their communities, spearheading social change.

Serjuntae's story

Serjuntae moved to the UK from Bermuda a few years ago. She found herself living in an area densely populated by Muslims and going to a school where she was one of only a few students with a Christian heritage. Some of the students at her school were hostile towards her because of her accent, presuming that she was American, and because she wasn't Muslim. (Some British Pakistanis don't like the USA because of their intervention in Islamic nations such as Iraq and Afghanistan.) This made her mother uneasy with Muslims, as she was upset that her daughter was struggling to fit in and make friends. However, Serjuntae quickly found The Feast and, as a result, gained the confidence to talk to her Muslim peers, becoming good friends with one girl in particular. She now has friends of all faiths and enjoys living in Birmingham and going to school. Her mum, too, through seeing Serjuntae become able to make friends with Muslims, has had her feelings towards them changed and is much more open to befriending them.

Where next for The Feast?

We expect to continue to set up new initiatives in various locations across the United Kingdom, and possibly further afield. There has been worldwide interest in our work, and agencies from across the globe have sent people to our training events to learn how to start relationship-building in their own situations. As we grow bigger, it is becoming necessary for local leaders to take The Feast into their context, as we cannot manage it all from our Birmingham office.

Training others in this sort of work has become a priority for us, as there have been many requests for us to do so. We're keen to see young people everywhere learn to share their faith and live in peace with their peers, and so we are running training days across the UK.

As we grow and develop, young people continue to be our focus. We think it of primary importance to continue running small youth events that help teenagers to befriend others and share their faith. It started because of them, and they need to remain our priority. We've seen that young people can lead and run their own events, and this is definitely a development that we want to pursue further.

Reaching out to other faith communities in your own context

Here are a few pointers for working successfully with young people from other faiths.

Be open and honest about your aims

Working with any young people is great: we learn a lot from them. Interfaith dialogue with young people is good for many reasons: it helps to build their confidence and make communities stronger and more peaceful. There is, of course, a desire in Christians to see young people learn about who Christ is, including young people from other faiths. It could be that you, or those you work with, would like to see the Hindu, Sikh and Muslim children around you become Christians. It is worth noting that there are some people of other faiths whose desire is just as strong to see you and Christian young people convert to their faith. After all, if they care about you and believe it's the best thing for you, of course they would want to convert you.

With this in mind, it's really important that any work that we Christians do with young people is done ethically, with great integrity and full awareness. If you are planning to include an evangelistic talk and an invitation for young people from other faiths to become Christians, you need to make it abundantly clear to them and their parents that this is what's going to happen. I severely doubt that they would attend, of course, just as it's unlikely that Christian children would be sent by their parents to a Muslim holiday club that was encouraging them to accept Islam. Working with young people of other faiths means treating them and their families as you would like to be treated yourself, allowing them the space and freedom to express and share their faith too, listening and taking it seriously. Therefore, running a Feast-style event, where you enable young people to talk and share on equal grounds, is a good and credible way to work with other faiths.

If you are clear about your motives and activities, and tell everyone the same story, you will incur respect and trust. If your story changes depending on who you're talking to—for example, telling Christians that you're proselytising but telling Muslims that you're not—this will win you no credibility. Always treat people of other faiths as you would want to be treated by them, as Jesus himself commanded (Luke 6:31).

Develop relationships with leaders

Good relationships with leaders or 'gatekeepers' of other faiths are vital. Sometimes these relationships take a long time to build, yet they are fundamental to any long-term work you might wish to pursue. The Feast was able to develop quickly because of the years of work that Andrew Smith had already done. It's not only important to have leaders on side; it's also beneficial to have them involved in the planning of any event. Always include at least one trustworthy adult from the faith of the young people attending an event. It might take time to develop those relationships, but it is well worthwhile to ensure longevity in the work you want to do.

Get the mix right

Make sure you have equal numbers of young people from each faith at your event. This way, no one gets left out. Don't be afraid to pre-set groups, and encourage others to work with people they don't know; these events are all about making relationships.

Work within the Guidelines for Dialogue

Help the young people to understand the Guidelines for Dialogue and the reasons why you're using them. Take time to get to know them yourself, too. Don't ignore it when a young person breaks the guidelines (or any other boundaries you have set in place).

Be sensitive

Make your event 'neutral', allowing all faiths to take part equally. Make provisions for prayer times if necessary, as well as dietary requirements and any other cultural considerations. Make sure that any music you play is acceptable to the different faiths taking part.

4

Rural bus ministry

Kerygma Trust works in Staffordshire and its adjoining counties. Through its specially fitted-out double-decker bus, it works with schools to provide lessons and collective worship, and with local communities, providing a space for young people where one might not otherwise exist. Using a bus in a rural context means that resources can reach those who have no access to youth provision as their village or community is too small to afford it.

Tina Taylor works with Youth for Christ in the South Lakes. South Lakes YFC run the Light Bus, a kitted-out double-decker bus which they take out to the community as a resource for local young people. It is used as a platform to share the gospel in word and in deed.

Kerygma Trust

Any project or work of outreach has to start somewhere or with someone, whether a group or an individual. It is born out of a desire or dream, sometimes called a vision. Some would add that such a scenario comes through a sense of calling, in response to a perceived need (or perhaps an inner frustration).

In the case of Kerygma, there was a sense of God giving to an individual a strong awareness of his presence and a challenge to a work yet to be launched. The individual was Colin Stephenson, an evangelist who had been working with Scripture Union in the West Midlands for many years. As part of his ongoing work and personal call, he had been praying that the Lord would reveal if there was anything else he should be doing or incorporating into his ministry. Those prayers were answered as Colin was driving on a stretch of the M25 close by Heathrow airport during January 2004, returning from a conference on the south coast.

'Reaching out to our nation's children' had been the main focus of the conference. There, Colin had met some delegates who had travelled up from Cornwall, and discovered through mutual interest and connections (Colin being from Cornwall himself) the great work that was being done in the county by different groups. In particular, he had heard of the prayer groups being set up with a focus on children and youth, and the work of the 'Good News Bus'.

It was hardly surprising that all these thoughts about the work in the south-west gathered momentum as Colin travelled on the orbital motorway, when God intervened and told him that what he was excited about in that part of the country could happen where he lived too. The seeds of

Kerygma were born in those moments and Colin was open to how the Lord was going to bring it about.

After a full two years with many issues to face and a team to gather, not least a working double-decker bus to find, the project finally became known as the Kerygma Bus Ministry, with the strapline 'Touching the heart of community'. At Easter 2006, the ministry kicked off in Stafford, using a Bristol VR Series 2 double-decker, which was replaced five years later by a Volvo City Bus.

A bus is a great visual outreach tool: you can't miss it, and most people have been on a bus of one kind or another, so it brings a feeling of familiarity. Surprisingly, though, many children have never been on a double-decker bus before, so therein lies a ready-made wow factor. Indeed, bus ministry is limited only by our imagination, and a place to be able to park it.

In 2011, after Colin had moved on from Scripture Union, the bus ministry continued, with a trust being set up to support his continuing work along with the volunteer team. The name by which it is now known is the Kerygma Community Outreach Trust. Each of these four words has been significant in the way that the work has developed and is integral to its operation.

First, the name Kerygma, which is usually used as short-hand for the project, comes from the root of a Greek word meaning 'to tell out or proclaim good news'. The name was chosen deliberately to describe what the project was going to do and to raise curiosity. Sure enough, it has broken the ice in many initial conversations, sparking questions like 'What does the name mean?' and 'What is the bus for?' Since 2006, Kerygma has been involved in a wide spectrum of events and locations, from village fêtes and car boot sales to town centre marketplaces and community events. It has been instrumental in establishing village youth work and has visited nearly 50 schools in the region to provide onboard RE lessons. These lessons have seen the team welcome over 10,000 children and staff on board—an amazing privilege. Many of the schools involved are in very rural settings and the arrival of a double-decker bus raises lots of excitement and anticipation—a schools worker's dream.

'Community' is a very inclusive word, widely used and accepted right across the spectrum in today's multicultural settings. It means different things to different groups who strive for 'community' wherever they live out their day-to-day lives, but it generally represents ideas about belonging and acceptance. Kerygma recognises all of this, and, from a faith perspective, believes that these are Christian ideals and goals to aim for. The goals are reflected in the updated strapline of the project: 'Bringing Communities Together'. All of this means that the project is highly visible and has to be worked out in the public domain. You can't easily hide a double-decker bus.

'Outreach' is a much-maligned and downgraded word in many people's thinking, especially within the Christian church. It can often carry the idea of uncomfortable situations in which Christians have to suffer great embarrassment as they rather reluctantly 'make a stand for their faith', whether through supporting an organised public event or through their own personal witness. However, the word is regularly used, for instance, in situations where secular and medical organisations have 'outreach workers'. It is very much connected to work in the community and has therefore redeemed itself in the present social climate.

That said, the word still does not invite similar sympathy

within the Christian community. It sits uncomfortably, for many people, alongside the word 'evangelism', which can also ring alarm bells. Kerygma's ethos is to work together as a team and to forge links within its sphere of influence to enable and assist churches or other groups in their locality. It seeks to be an active and visible presence wherever it goes, a 'light that cannot be hidden with a message that desperately needs to be heard'—a welcome friend and ambassador to all in sharing good news.

So, with the good news of God's love to share, through both presence and proclamation, Kerygma Community Outreach seeks to develop the work of the 'Trust'. This in turn seeks to encourage and support the resource requirements for the overall ministry. While Kerygma is set up as a Trust with charitable and company status, which carries the overall responsibility of 'keeping the wheels turning', it is essentially about people. These people have come together and have committed themselves to the mission, as they follow not just one man's aspirations or calling, but the voice of the Holy Spirit.

Out and about

Hixon is a village that lies approximately eight miles to the east of Stafford. In 2006, the first visit was made there, with the original bus, to reach out to young people. There had been rumours of vandalism in the village, and negative press reports. Regular visits continued for several weeks on a Tuesday evening over a summer period with virtually no response. A prayer and discussion evening was called and, as the team met, it was decided that three more weeks would be given to the visits to see if any change would occur. Seven years later, and with scores of young people boarding the bus over those years, the Tuesday night visits still take place in school term times, with an average attendance of nearly 30 young people each week. What a blessing those extra three weeks' grace eventually turned out to be!

Tuesday night, for many of the youth in the village, is definitely 'Kerygma Night'. During the summer, instead of having the bus, a gazebo is erected on the local sports ground, attracting young people for games and snacks. The bus visits recommence when the autumn school term begins, and they continue throughout the winter. It is a welcome drop-in place, offering light crafts, table-top games and computer games and quizzes as regular activities. Each week a message is shared by one of the team or an invited visitor. This is commonly known as 'the God slot' or simply 'talk time' and, though it isn't compulsory, most people do climb the stairs to the upper deck to take part. The message closes with a prayer and often an invitation to pray, chat further or ask questions. Sometimes prayer requests are written down and posted in the 'Kerygma Prayer Box', to be offered in prayer by the team at the end of the evening.

One of the emerging young leaders in the current group has been confirmed within her church tradition in recent months, and part of her personal story is the positive influence that Kerygma on a Tuesday night has had on her. Kerygma continues to be the only visible youth work in the immediate area. This is a testimony to the faithful work of the various team members who have regularly travelled the 16-mile round trip each week since 2006. The local vicar visits the bus most weeks and has been a real encouragement to the team. He also makes the church available over the summer period if the weather is wet.

Such is the trust put in the Kerygma visits that parents will chat freely to the team as they drop off and collect their young people. This is great for all concerned, as it enables people to get to know each other better and build up a deeper trust. As the work in Hixon village has gone so well, there is no current exit strategy. The door of opportunity here remains fully open and the seeds of the gospel are continually being sown. The story is still unfolding.

The question may be asked, 'Is all village work like this?' Quite plainly, it is not. At a neighbouring village, where the bus team worked for over a year on another evening in the week, it did not become established. Despite various attempts and discussion, it has ceased to be a viable ministry at this present time. Sometimes we have to acknowledge that there are 'seasons' of opportunity in outreach work. Whether one of these 'seasons' will arise in the future remains to be seen.

Schools work

Schools work is a great privilege, whether in a rural setting or in larger urban areas. Many thousands of young people have been on board the Kerygma bus during its schools outreach in local communities. Particularly in smaller communities, any event at the local school becomes a real highlight. On one such occasion, attendance doubled to 60 with a visit from a larger urban school. When the 30 town children looked out of the upper deck windows, they were very excited to see the sheep and cows in the next field.

Depending on the size of the school, visits can be spread over more than one day. Not only do these occasions generate great excitement for the children, but teachers are also encouraged by a team of dedicated and caring volunteers. In the main, the schools attended are primary schools, although we keep the options open for any school to be included. Visits to high schools and special needs schools have all taken place in the course of Kerygma's history.

Lesson planning is always a joint exercise between a school staff member and the leader of the team, and happens in conjunction with the site visit, which has to take place before the bus arrives on the planned date. Access, parking and safety all have to be taken into consideration at each location, and the route has to be checked out for low bridges, overhanging trees and narrow lanes. The lessons often come out of the school's requirements from the curriculum, the season of the year, or, on occasion, an invitation for the team to present their own choice of material. The topics always have a biblical base as their framework. Themes are explored using as much interactivity as possible, including games, quizzes, music, video, storytelling, puppets, discussion, Q&A, fun sheets and so on.

The bus has also been set up as a prayer space, allowing children to explore various themes using their own senses and feelings—a kind of activity that they might not have experienced before. This approach, which highlights spirituality, has gathered momentum over the past couple of years, not only within schools themselves but in the wider areas of RE education and inspection. One RE teacher in a middle school commented, 'The visit was a valuable and unique way of delivering a global message of harmony.'

Future plans and new opportunities

In the immediate future, Kerygma plans to do more of the same, but there is the capacity for the bus to be used more widely in schools and churches within the region. The team certainly have a passion to see this great tool being used even more significantly. Budgets are tight in the schools context, as in many places during the current financial climate. However, in faith, the work continues.

The Trust is developing closer ties with local churches in order to promote mutual support and develop awareness of how we might help and encourage churches in reaching out to people on their own doorstep. There is always the need, too, for new volunteer team members who can be involved in a variety of ways to complement the whole ministry.

Although it is centred on the bus, Kerygma's work is not a 'one trick' ministry. Children and youth are a high-priority focus, but the team is always open to developing new and varied projects. Two of these new opportunities are in the early stages at the time of writing. One is to provide the bus as a drop-in facility to a local organisation called 'Signposts', which has a Christian ethos and is essentially a support centre for people in the community, offering counselling, drug awareness, computer and training facilities and financial advice. Kerygma has been asked to provide the bus on a twice-monthly basis on an estate in Barlaston. There are no meeting places on the estate, so a good-sized bus will be an excellent facility in this setting.

The second project is to maximise the use of the bus itself by offering it as a 'Drive the Bus Experience'. This will give anyone with a current full driving licence the opportunity to drive the bus themselves in a safe environment on a local airfield, supported by a qualified instructor. It will help to raise some finance to support the ministry and will provide that 'I'd love to drive a bus someday' dream experience. It could even encourage some to consider training to become one of the team's drivers. Drivers are, of course, essential for a bus ministry, so the initiative will help to raise the profile for this important role.

Useful contacts

- Associated Bus Ministries has a list of most of the bus or mobile projects in the country that are used exclusively for mission outreach.
- Membership of 'Working on Wheels' (the working title of the National Playbus Association) is highly recommended.
- Church Army has several buses around the country and can offer advice from experienced practitioners.
- Kerygma Community Outreach Trust and Colin Stephenson: email kerygma@hotmail.co.uk, or visit the website www.kerygmatrust.co.uk

The Light Bus

In 2005, a local man had a vision that all the churches in the South Lakes community would work together to share the gospel of the Lord Jesus Christ with the youth in the area. A group of volunteers from the churches of Windermere, Bowness and Ambleside began to meet to discuss how this could be achieved, and it was decided that placing the vision under the banner of Youth for Christ would help to strengthen its evangelical focus. In 2007, the charity South Lakes Youth for Christ was formed.

You would assume that, in order to do 'youth work', a youth worker would be needed, and that is precisely the initial step that SLYFC took. Once a suitable employee was found, it didn't take long to discover that the task of fulfilling this large and fairly undefined vision was too much for one individual. Small inroads were made, but, when we found ourselves in a position to readvertise the post, it seemed clear that either there would have to be an operational change or we would have to set aside the project altogether.

It was at this stage, after four years of meeting as trustees, that a focus on prayer began to emerge. Monthly prayer meetings were held around the churches represented as we sought the direction of the Holy Spirit. It was, we believe, through prayer that members of local churches began to be stirred in their hearts, to catch the vision and respond to the call of the Lord to reach out to the young people in our community. Prayer has increased and continues to be the lifeline in all that we do.

Out of this atmosphere of prayer, one of the trustees had a vision that the Lord wanted us to operate our youth ministry from a double-decker bus. It was a matter of days before an appropriately equipped vehicle was found. The Light Bus, previously owned by a lighting company and used for exhibitions, was perfect for our purpose. We had just enough money to buy the bus but, of course, there were questions to be answered, doubts to be faced and fears to be conquered. Above all else, it seemed that the Lord desired the churches to work as one and he was prepared to wait until we worked it out together. We prayed and, in December 2012, took the bold and unanimous decision to purchase the Light Bus.

After some further work on the bus, safeguarding training, CRB checks, local permissions and more prayer, the Light Bus was ready for action. We drive the bus to a district council car park in Windermere every Friday, pray for 15 minutes and then open the doors to the young people of the community. We are not youth workers but our pool of 20 volunteers has a heart to get alongside the young people and to build relationships with them. The bus is an instant draw and we welcome between 20 and 60 young people each week. They now wait expectantly for us to arrive at the car park.

Initially we felt that we would be ministering to the over-15s, but, from the outset, the age range stretched from 8 to 20, and we did not feel it was right to turn any of them away. Of course, this extensive age range has brought its own challenges. We have found that we need to put in some structure for the younger children, with specific games, craft activities, regular hot chocolate time and DVDs. Although the bus has X-box and large screen facilities, the older ones tend to chat and play interactive games such as Uno or Rapidough. Although we do not discourage the older group to come on board the bus between 7.30 and 9 pm, when the younger ones are there, they know that they have exclusive use of the bus from 9 pm onwards, when we make hot drinks for them, play games and chat. Trust and friendships are being established. We have recently initiated a 'Talk2…' session, where we ask a member of the community or church to come and talk to the young people and invite questions. While we do not overtly preach the gospel each week, the young people know that we are Christians and that we are happy to answer their questions. The team's constancy and love towards them communicates the gospel in a very practical manner, often without words.

This project is very much in its infancy. We do not plan months in advance, as we are discovering that God unfolds his plan gradually on a 'need to know' basis. The Light Bus has been used in a variety of settings as well as for our weekly Friday slot. If we receive an invitation and are persuaded that it is in keeping with God's plan for the bus, and provided that our hosts have an appropriate team to support the ministry they are suggesting, we are happy to take the Light Bus anywhere within the South Lakes area of operation.

It's a little too soon in the life of the ministry to discern any long-term impact on the children and young people who join us on the bus, but relationships are strengthening and the children and young people are very open to Christianity and prayer.

We are constantly amazed at how God works through prayer, the unity of the local churches, a double-decker bus and a bunch of unqualified volunteers in order to draw young people to himself. 'O how great are God's riches and wisdom and knowledge! How impossible it is for us to understand his decisions and his ways!' (Romans 11:33, NLT).

Bus ministry in your own context

- If you are interested in 'mobile ministry' and believe that it could be helpful in your setting, seek the Lord and seek the help of others, in that order. This was the way Kerygma began—as one person wrestling with a passion and a burden, sensing what God was saying. Invite others to share in the vision, even if everyone doesn't fully understand where it might lead. In Kerygma's case, over 40 people started to meet and pray on a monthly basis for the establishment of the ministry, long before any bus had been obtained.

- Colin Stephenson personally visited several mobile projects to get a much more hands-on feel of what was involved. This experience was both informative and inspirational to the wider group. Recognise that there is expert advice and wisdom available, to tell you where to begin and how to set your project up. This kind of advice will let you know what is best *not* to do as well as giving you the information you need. Setting up a bus ministry should not be taken lightly: it will involve a lot of time.

- Be aware of the financial implications of setting up such a project.
- Be as sure as possible of what you believe God wants, and appreciate all the wisdom and experience of those who are already involved and can help you. Have a plan, but make sure it is very flexible.
- Pray through everything—the big picture and the details—and pray often. Children and youth accept prayer and are intrigued by it.
- Work at keeping unity between all the churches in the area. In addition, build good relationships with the police and local authorities; they can be very supportive.
- Primary-aged children work better with structure, and for all ages it's important to have boundaries, without imposing strict rules.
- It takes time to build trust, so be prepared to put in the hours just being with the young people to form those relationships.
- Have fun: it's infectious.
- Interactive, non-electronic games work best, as they give plenty of space for conversation and interaction.

5

Celebrate Life

Tessa Oram has worked for Faith in Education for nine years. The organisation was set up in response to local church concern that Hull had had the worst school league table results in the country for many years running, and the reputation of schools in the city was low. Tessa works as a York Diocesan employee but is externally funded, entirely through gifts and grants. Her remit is to build links between schools and churches, with the aim of raising aspiration and bringing an extra stream of resource into the schools.

Tessa has experimented with many ways of surprising schools with the relevance of the church, and here she tells the story of mentoring, which is the current flourishing expression of Christian involvement in schools across the city.

Education in Hull

Debby and the head of pastoral care stood watching the doorway anxiously. Paige had promised to attend her mentoring session but was nowhere to be seen. All the other mentors had settled themselves into their rooms with their students and were starting their session. Then, as they watched, a taxi drew up into the school playground and, with a flick of her long dyed black hair, Paige jumped out of the car, paid the driver and rushed into the Learning Support block to meet Debby. She had a huge grin and looked as if she wanted to hug her mentor, remembering just in time how uncool that would be in school.

The chatter started immediately as they made their way to their own space, with the mentoring pack bulging with creative activities and a few edible treats waiting to be discovered in the course of the session. The teacher turned to me with a look of disbelief on her face. 'It is a total miracle,' she said. Paige, a known school refuser—a girl with shoulders bowed from carrying a pile of impossibly complex problems thus far in her short 15 years, and an attitude of disdain towards every teacher in the failing school—had used her own money to take a taxi to ensure she didn't miss a minute of her mentoring session!

I had worked as Faith in Education worker in Hull for six years and had just said a sad farewell to Julia, a co-worker with the same vision as I had, to bring the light of God into the darkest places of Hull. Together we had taken risks, finding ourselves in strange marginal places—in squats and hostels, in schools where we had asked for 'your ten naughtiest pupils', and in Edinburgh, finding out how to fix rickshaws with a group of homeless young people. We had worked hard and close, and now it was over. Julia had gone to Hong Kong while I was left in Hull, a bit more tired and a bit less naive than I had been when I arrived. I still had the desire to find real, relevant ways to reach the 'bottom of the pile', to get a chance to say to as many discarded kids as I could that they had been created by one who knew them, planned them, loved them and had so much in store for them. Yet, on my own now, I couldn't see how I could do it.

I'd stumbled across a mentoring seminar that summer at New Wine North. I had popped into the seminar to get out of the rain, but, as the idea opened up, I'd realised that this was the way forward, with some tweaks and adaptations, for my work in Hull. My broad job description was to find ways for Christians in Hull to get involved in education. Mentoring seemed to be the bit of thread I was looking for, so I grabbed hold of it and am still discovering where it leads.

Hull has always had a bit of a problem with its reputation. Named as the crappiest place to live in the UK, some parts of the city have believed that lie, and some parts just haven't understood the great resources that they have within them. Education has always suffered. Being stuck at the bottom of league tables, awful results, badly designed schools, a fear of being unable to recruit or retain good staff—all have combined to put a curse on the schools. My role was created to throw the church's hat into the ring as part of the city's fight to raise aspiration, reputation and achievement.

Offering something different

It became clear that mentoring was a way to bring Christians into schools to offer something life-enhancing, helpful and possibly multidimensional to a small handful of students in our city. My first job was to collect a bunch of willing volunteers. My secret for collecting potential mentors is simple, and many people are sceptical when I say that I never recruit, as the team is large, flourishing and ever increasing. In the church context especially, there are always demands on people's time, energy and money, and I hate the use of guilt and manipulation to get people to do things. I decided early on that there would be no website, no posters and no recruitment drive. Instead, I would simply tell the story of young people, broken by their experiences, finding themselves in situations not of their own making—poverty, sadness, trauma and neglect. Their needs result in behaviour that gives school headaches, because there are no spare resources to help them. It's a story, too, of a God who sees these people at the bottom of the pile, loves them and regards them as his favourites. It's about digging for diamonds in the dirt pile. As I tell the story, sometimes it resonates with a soul who is already crying out for the poor and broken but has not yet found ways of accessing them to offer help. And as the stories chime together, my team is built.

The team is made up of people from across a large geographical area and represents all flavours of church tradition. It must be said that churches are very underpopulated in Hull. At one time, the city claimed the lowest church attendance in the country and, from my perspective, coming from London, I was shocked at how far 'behind' the rest of the country the expression of church seemed to be. However, despite the low numbers and the lack of resources, there are faithful, humble people who want to see the kingdom of God come. The denomination doesn't matter, and nor does the volunteer's level of experience. It's the heart I am after, and, after a few sessions with the rest of the team, a new mentor will know very quickly if it is the kind of activity that will work for them.

We started with one school and a team of six. In many ways, we made it up as we went along. The first few weeks were exhilarating as, together, we pushed through an invisible wall—the lack of regular Christian presence in secondary schools—which, to our knowledge, had not been breached before. We met together as a team for three sessions, getting to know each other, talking about how we were going to mentor and familiarising ourselves with the material. We were very different in terms of age, gender, church and life experience, but we all wanted to meet the students that the school had allocated us.

Starting with a school

We call the project Celebrate Life, and the approach to the school goes like this. I make an appointment to see the head teacher and explain that we have a mentoring team available to come into the school. I make it clear at the start that the project is free of charge to the school and is funded by donations to Faith in Education. The 'gift' aspect is vital. It means that we owe the school nothing: we are free agents and we can determine what we can give and when. It is also a work of grace and not an obligation, which liberates every part of what we do.

No school has ever wondered about the origin of the work. Some have asked whether we intend to 'evangelise', to which I reply that we are all Christians on the team and will answer questions about our faith if asked. However, our aim in the school is not to try to convert anyone; rather, we express our values in the way we work. To be able to mention the

Church of England gives me a 'place to stand', although I am not sure it gives any particular credibility within the school. A stand-alone group of Christians wanting to do similar work will need to have an umbrella for their own accountability and best practice, but my experience is that schools extend a welcome to groups that are reliable, sensitive and accommodating, rather than needing 'proof of pedigree'.

I explain that, as we are about 'celebrating life', we want the school to identify students for whom no one celebrates their existence. Always, as I say this, I have a lump in my throat—not because of sadness, but because I fear that I have pushed it too far, that I am living in sentimentality or some kind of Victorian-style philanthropy. Nevertheless, the head teacher always nods and declares that they have at least a dozen names in mind already. The sad fact is that, even in today's hi-tech, advanced society, there are children who are not celebrated.

We ask the school to identify the students, and then, once we have the names, we ask for no other background information. This is a shocker—both the school and the mentor usually want as much background as they can get—but I stand firm against it. Knowledge is power, and each student will have a file as thick as a cereal box full of reports, evaluations, judgements, opinions, assessments and targets, all of which are someone else's subjective opinions. We don't want to meet the mentee with power over them. We don't want to meet a reputation; we want to give the students a chance to meet us as equally and fairly as possible. We want our encounter to be about grace, not fear. Hence, no background, ever.

I go on to explain that we come into school as a team, usually four or five of us. Any bigger and the school would not have space to accommodate us; any smaller and we'd be overstretched and isolated. We come armed with resource packs—a bag full of sticky tape, pens, glue, wet wipes, a play mat and scissors—and four different creative activities with which to engage the mentee. These activities vary: we write two curriculums for a year, one for primary-age children and one for the secondary age group. They range from games to making things, to experiments, to puzzles, to choosing activities, to 'gratitude marbles': there are so many different activities, aimed at either gender and pretty much across the age range. We are totally self-contained with our resources, bringing everything we might need, including bottles of water and bags for carrying things home. There is no trace of our work after we have gone.

What we do

The curriculum is based loosely on Christian values and enables mentors to spend time getting to know the mentee and their situation, talking about what makes them tick and how they react in different situations. Three or four questions go with each session, but there is nothing direct about the questioning or the subject matter. Each session comes at the 'issue' from an angle, with questions carefully constructed to open up a conversation and still give the mentee an element of choice about their level of disclosure. For example, on the subject of anger, one of the questions is 'If you were head teacher of this school, what would you change first?' This can be answered on many levels, from 'the colour of the classrooms' (a 'safe' reply) to 'a stricter bullying policy', which might lead to a further disclosure of bullying experiences and frustrations about how they are dealt with.

Mentors are instructed about the use of the activities resource pack: it is there as a tool for them to use, they do not have to adhere strictly to it, and, if the conversation takes off in a different direction, that is fine. Our aim is always to establish a relationship of trust and affirmation, to listen and provide space. We have a 'light touch', trying to bring a bit of peace and joy into lives that are often troubled and traumatised. We make clear to the school and the mentee that it is a voluntary relationship: we are not there to discipline, assess or evaluate the mentee in any way.

We also stress that nothing we discuss will ever be revealed to the mentee's peers. This seems to be the most pressing concern in young people's minds. We never promise total confidentiality, though, as we need to leave space to be able to talk over issues and challenges as a team, to pray over them and work out how best to approach particular difficulties. We also, obviously, need a safeguarding route back to the school, to be able to talk about anything that we feel must be passed on. Fresh disclosures of abuse must be addressed in accordance with an established safeguarding procedure. However, our experience is that most of the conversations we have are about topics that are already known to social services, the school and sometimes the police. We truly offer a safe place where mentees can process some of the stuff that 'authorities' are dealing with, yet for which no pastoral provision has been made.

The impact we have seen over the past few years of mentoring has been both significant and hidden. We have had a few moments of total surprise, like the experience with Paige, described at the start of this chapter. Then there was 15-year-old Brandon, who sat in a room with his 75-year-old mentor, Anne, week in, week out, hardly speaking. Sometimes he would engage with making a tiny motorbike kit; sometimes he would sticky-tape up the room and kick chairs over. Anne would bring in her homemade chocolate fridge cake and just sat with him, a calm presence. Brandon cried when the mentoring year was over. When we held an end-of-term party, he hid in the bushes outside the venue, waiting to see Anne as she came out to load her car.

Throughout our work, we have noticed changes in our mentees' appearance, attitude, facial hardness and ability to laugh, as well as their reputation among peers and staff. We have seen warm attached relationships develop, which we maintain as far as we can, through parties and residentials.

Celebrating life

The parties we hold every term provide space for this continuation of relationship and also allow us to extend our arms to the families and friends of our mentees. We have learnt that, to throw a party that works, which is valued by those we want to come, we must throw off any social norms and welcome those who would never usually attend an event. We talk about the party consistently for about six weeks before it happens, issuing new printed invitations at each conversation. We get phone numbers, where we can, for a reminder on the day, and organise transport from around the city. Everything is free, and we throw as much as possible of the available resources into ensuring that the party suits the guests.

In the past, we have held a KFC picnic, organised big tables of crafts and activities accessible to all, put together a sweet-and-ice-cream factory, and provided quiet corners and noisy games. The tone of the party is usually quiet but busy. We always find some way of communicating God's love in a more upfront way than we can do in school. We have made Easter gardens, asked the bishop to pray a blessing, engaged an actress to role-play Mary Magdalene, and invited a body-popper with a story, fire eaters, Christian rappers and Christian magicians. The visit of the local actress who played Mary really stands out. In a monologue she described how she had seen Jesus killed and then raised from the dead. She did it in a low-key but very powerful way—conversational yet fairly hard-hitting. As soon as she started to talk, a group of girls started running round the hall, screaming and laughing. This was, of course, a concern, but we have learnt to look for what God is doing, rather than focus on what is not happening. Another small group of girls sat in front of 'Mary', intently listening. At the end they asked if they could meet her—and they stayed chatting for a long time. Two weeks after Easter, we heard that one of this small responsive group had died on Holy Saturday. It was a shock to us all, but also a vivid reminder of the value of the work we are doing and the window of opportunity that we have been given.

One of the unexpected consequences of the work has been the value of the friendships, support, pastoral help, prayer and courage that we find together as a mentoring team. No one came into the mentoring project to make friends or to be encouraged in their own lives, but that is surely what has happened. The work is not high-profile or flashy in any way. We sit in a corner of a school with a 'bottom of the pile' student, doing very detailed craft activities and talking mainly about very mundane things—yet God uses the 'fish and loaves' that we offer and brings much increase.

Ben's story

The first time we met Ben, I thought that there had been a mistake. He was tiny, blond, blue-eyed, extremely polite and quiet. Assured by the school that Ben was indeed the intended mentee, we started a relationship with him that became key in his life. Over four years, he was mentored by a couple of people, notably by Dave. Dave had a talent for engaging Ben with light banter and an exploration of all things mechanical and quirky. He was also a sounding-board for Ben to unpack some of his troubles.

Ben was left confused and devastated when his dad was put in prison. On his dad's release, there was an injunction preventing him from seeing his children, yet Ben found him and visited him as often as he could, which eventually led to his dad's re-arrest. His mum could not handle the six kids or the trauma and was finding refuge in alcohol. It was left to his grandparents to look after him, which they were doing as well as they could. Ben fell foul of school many times. He was unable to concentrate and had a mind full of other things. We often had to claim him from the Red Room—the exclusion room—for his mentoring sessions.

Ben responded well to all the mentoring activities and conversation. He never failed to turn up, even when excluded, and engaged in creativity and games as if his life depended on it. I remember him making the most fantastic game of blow-football from a piece of cardboard and an orange net, two straws and a pingpong ball. He built kits, devised games and played cards.

One day he came to school out of uniform, saying that his house had been burnt down. The school seemed to verify his claim, with the additional information that there had been no insurance. We had a whipround among the mentoring team and bought Ben a new set of uniform, shoes, school bag and pens. The school was blown away by this act, although we played it down as much as we could. Ben was equally impressed and tried on the clothes right there. We never saw them again: he never wore any of what we had bought or, indeed, used any of the school equipment. We have no idea what happened to them. We prayed that God would use the gesture to bless the family.

When we invited Ben to a weekend away that we ran for all the mentees, he responded with extreme enthusiasm—and then we began to see at first-hand why the school had sent him to us as a mentee. He was unable to conform to even the most basic patterns of life and we were challenged to the limits by him. He packed his bag and attempted to walk home twice, broke a window and caused all kinds of trouble and trauma. He refused to eat (despite showing signs of malnourishment) and would not engage in any of the organised activities, choosing instead to climb the climbing tower at midnight, alone, and putting most of his energy into lighting fires with deodorant cans. By the end of the weekend, we were shattered in every way and feared for the continuation of our relationships with the mentees, especially Ben. The next time we saw him, he came running up to us, begging us for another 'holiday' and declaring to all who would listen that the weekend had been the best time of his life.

Ben attended every party we organised, usually with many small siblings in tow, and came to the last party with not just his siblings but also his mum. This was a major breakthrough—that his mum, who was shunned and blamed by society and lived as a recluse, trusted us enough to come to our social event and chat quite happily.

Ben is no longer mentored by us. It is hard to evaluate the impact of a mentoring relationship and we resist offering any evaluation to the school. How do you track a packet of seeds scattered in a garden? Much of what has been sown into Ben's life through this precious time with a reliable and trustworthy adult, who speaks truth and hope every week in a gentle and kind way, may not come to fruition for years.

We didn't turn Ben's life around, we didn't save him from exclusion from school, we didn't sort him or his family out, and we didn't see improved grades or open up further educational opportunities for him. We did, however, provide a safe place for him to be accepted for who he is, without pressure to perform or improve, where he could make jokes, play games and catch up with childhood experiences that he had missed. We gave him a chance to talk, explore his experiences and look at his choices. We gave him a community to belong to that was rooting for him, and we expressed God's love to him in a tangible way. We were able to be an oasis for Ben, an hour a week for four years, as he struggled through the brokenness of a traumatic life. We also covered Ben and his family in prayer, believing words of life for him, listening to God for him and speaking prophetically about him. The fact is that as soon as we met Ben and asked for the kingdom of God to come in his life, and walked with him faithfully, we collaborated with God in ensuring that his life would never be the same. We now trust him into God's hands with grateful thanks, and listen out for any news of what he does next.

The names in this story have been changed.

Mentoring in your own context

Here are some tips and advice on exploring a mentoring project:

- Start small. Gather a team of about six, tell the story, share the vision of how mentoring can transform people and, most importantly, pray.
- Approach one school to start with, asking to meet the head teacher.
- Get an administration system in place. You need an application form for the mentor and two references, as well as a way of processing DBS (Disclosure and Barring Service) forms. Schools will not allow you in to do anything without an up-to-date DBS form, so this is essential.
- A volunteer contract is a good tool to ensure that there are no misunderstandings. Make sure everyone knows who is the person who talks to the school: having more than one 'lead person' makes things very messy.
- Expect to waste your time. Sometimes a team will meet, pray, eat, gear up, go into school with a pack of carefully constructed resources, and only one mentee will be there. Perhaps the school will have exams on, but no one thought to tell you.
- Serve the school. Remember that your role is to bless the school, never to criticise what you see there. The school needs to know that you are on their side.
- Party with your people. Spend time as a team, eating together, talking, planning, praying and socialising. It all helps to build community, which is what mentoring is really all about.

- The leader needs to lead—to take responsibility and shoulder as much of the boring stuff as possible, to make it a light and easy role in which the volunteers can thrive. I have an assistant who works with me to prepare the packs and lead some of the teams. Recruiting a deputy is very important, to give you someone to talk things through with, make decisions with and share the load on a practical level.

6

The Lab

James Henley is Team Leader at The Lab in Newport, South Wales. The Lab is a community of missional people, groups and initiatives. It seeks to grow new forms of church with those who have little or no church background, to serve local communities and to develop young leaders. Made up of several different communities across the town, The Lab aims to reimagine spirituality and worship for their local context.

Experimental mission with young adults

The Lab has been experimenting with church and mission in Newport, South Wales, since 2006. Our journey began when a team led by Revd Justin Groves began drawing people together to meet on a Sunday night. A core group of young adults emerged, who were looking to do church in a different way.

Since we began, we've tried out several different venues, from church halls to the upper room of a pub, and are now meeting in some office space above a nail bar in the city centre. People have come and gone and the community has grown to about 20–30 people, mostly young adults between the ages of 16 and 30. We've seen several young people and young adults make some kind of commitment to faith over the last five years, and seen lots of others find a place to belong and be supported.

It's been a huge privilege to be a part of what God has been doing among young adults in Newport. The last seven years have been an incredible journey, where I've got to know and serve alongside some brilliant young people. We've made an awful lot of mistakes along the way, but we've also, mainly through our mistakes, failures and flukes, learned some important lessons about engaging with young adults who have little or no previous church background.

Over the years, we've created a number of different events, projects and groups that have helped our young adult ministry to develop. Our vision has been to develop The Lab in three main areas, which match our three values: relationships, reflection and reaction.

Relationships: loving and serving

Since The Lab first formed, we've found several different ways to try to engage with the student and young adult community in Newport. Our approach with these different forms of 'outreach' has always been to love and serve, making an intentional effort to build relationships with people outside the church, accepting and valuing them for who they are. We seek to share the gospel through our lives and actions first, praying for opportunities to share it through our words later.

Our initial attempt was through an event called 'Stuffed', where we invited students to an all-you-can-eat meal on a Wednesday night, before they went out clubbing later in the evening. Our supporting church, St Paul's, had a building with a fantastic kitchen and café area, which they generously allowed us to use, and we found a supportive older couple with lots of catering experience who offered to run the kitchen for us. At the beginning of the university year, we showered the university with flyers advertising what we were doing, and even handed out free samples of home-cooked chilli to entice students along. The first term was successful, but we quickly discovered that blanket marketing was much, much less effective than word-of-mouth, with friends inviting friends to come along.

After the first term, the couple who'd given their time to cook for us were unable to continue. However, we found that many of the young adults in our community and their friends were happy to help out in the kitchen and would relish the chance to bring together a meal for everyone else. At the start of the next term, we made a sign-up list and continued eating together each week. Over time, much more of an extended-family atmosphere emerged than we'd originally intended, and these Wednesday nights eventually evolved into our weekly community meal together.

We also realised that many of our group were talented musicians, and some were even writing and recording their own songs. When a friend of a friend started an open mic night in a local bar, this also became a natural gathering point for our community and a point of intersection with those outside of the church. After the event finished, several incredibly talented members of our community came together to run some open mic nights using the café space at St Paul's, inviting various musician friends to join us.

It's amazing how far the social networks of young adults can stretch. One open mic night was even attended by a young guy called Ed Sheeran, whom some of the guys had seen perform in London and invited along. About six months later, Ed was signed to a record label and recording his debut album, but one of his early performances was to a random group of young adults in a church in Newport.

Sarah's story

I've often heard the phrase 'believing, behaving, belonging' used to describe the process of evangelism and discipleship that happens through the church. First, people choose to make a commitment to 'believe'; then, as a result of their belief, they begin to 'behave' differently. Finally they find a place of 'belonging' within the church family. With young adults, my experience has been that this process most often happens in reverse. It's a process of 'belonging, behaving, believing', by which people who have joined The Lab first find a family where they can 'belong'. These positive friendships then have an influence on the way they are 'behaving', which leads them finally to a place of choosing to 'believe' and put their faith in Jesus.

Sarah and Tom both started university in Newport at the same time and moved into rooms just along the hallway from each other in the hall of residence. While Sarah had no church background whatsoever and was quite cynical about faith, Tom was a committed Christian who got involved in the university's Christian Union and started coming along to our Lab events. Sarah and Tom quickly got to know each other well, and Tom started inviting Sarah along to events such as our weekly community meal and an Alpha course that the CU were running.

When the Alpha course ended, Sarah felt that she'd met a lot of great people and found out a lot about Christianity, but didn't want to become a Christian. She was interested in the idea of God but still had a lot of questions left about what she believed.

However, the friendships Sarah had made within the CU and The Lab continued to grow and deepen, and soon Sarah felt very strongly part of our community. Over time, as a result of her friendships, she realised that some of her behaviour had begun to change as well. She had actively decided to try to follow Jesus' example of loving others. She began to realise that, since a lot of her friends were Christian, and she'd started to behave a lot like a Christian, perhaps that meant she was a Christian. The final step was to make a commitment to follow Jesus, and Sarah was baptised, surrounded by a crowd of supportive friends, on the beach on a cold spring afternoon.

Reflection: exploring spirituality and discipleship

Our Sunday worship gathering, now called 'The Cwtch' (*cwtch* is Welsh for a hug or a safe hiding place), is about creating a safe and honest space for students and young adults to grow spiritually together. Each week's gathering is different, led by different young adults from within our community. A typical gathering might include some acoustic-style sung worship (often involving obscure folk instruments like the ukulele, mandolin and melodica), some form of spoken liturgy, a group discussion or debate, and some form of creative prayer—all around a particular theme or Bible passage. Every four to six weeks, a local Methodist minister joins us to celebrate Communion.

In addition to the Sunday night meeting, we've experimented with many different ways of exploring discipleship together. As The Lab grew numerically, it became more and more difficult to sustain our community meal. It was a lot easier to prepare and cook a meal for the 10–15 people who were coming along when we started than the 25–30 who were now showing up each week. So we decided to split into small groups, with the hope that these groups might continue to cultivate a sense of belonging and mutual support and also offer more opportunities for our community to reflect theologically and study the Bible together.

Kahla's story

One of our small groups ended up being hosted by a couple of girls who were living in a shared house, with the group getting together for one evening a week. This was intriguing for one of the other girls living in the house, Kahla, who had no previous experience of church. Being very sociable, she was drawn into the life of the small group, listening carefully and asking lots of questions. She was invited to join us for our Lab weekend away, which happened in February. There, she was able to hear more of what it meant to follow Jesus. In the lead-up to the period of Lent, a conversation was struck up about whether people were planning to give something up for Lent or to do something special to help them focus on God.

It was then that Kahla made the decision to 'give up unbelief' for Lent—to push aside her sense of scepticism in order to try out following Jesus and see what it was like. From that point, Kahla made a huge step forward into the life of our community and towards relationship with God. Although she has since moved on in order to find work, her journey while she was part of The Lab was enormously significant.

Reaction: growing leaders and engaging in mission

About five years ago, a group of us were looking for somewhere to live and had a desire to experiment with living intentionally as a community on mission. We approached the Bishop of Monmouth and he offered us an unused vicarage on the Alway estate, an area of deprivation on the eastern edge of Newport. The community in Alway has continued to grow as we've experimented with rhythms of life and prayer and developed different initiatives to serve the local community, especially local young people. Out of this, we developed an apprenticeship scheme by which young adults, some from our community and some from elsewhere, join us for a year to be part of our team in Alway and develop in leadership and discipleship.

In September 2012, my wife Amy and I moved across Newport in order to try to grow community and church on the Duffryn estate. Duffryn is in the top three per cent of deprived areas in Wales. More recently, two of the girls in our Lab community decided to start a project called 'Eli Music', providing opportunities for children from difficult backgrounds to express themselves through music.

The Lab is evolving more and more into a network of different pioneering communities, initiatives and people all connected by mutual support and relationships. Local councillors and community associations have also recognised the contribution we've made and have given The Lab a couple of awards for some of our projects serving the local community.

Troy's story

Troy, aged 14, was one of the first guys we met when we moved into the Alway estate. While he was incredibly outgoing, charismatic and open to getting to know us, we were aware that, for his school, Troy was a bit of a problem. It didn't know what to do with him or how to engage his interest. School just wasn't for him.

We quickly realised that we had nothing to offer young people like Troy, except for long-term relationship and support. We didn't have any expert skills or a fancy programme to get young people back on track. What we could do, though, was to be there for them, listen to their problems and keep believing in them, no matter what else was happening in their lives.

Over five years, we've seen Troy develop from a fun-loving, fairly immature teenager into a responsible, inspirational young man. He's been through incredibly tough times, struggling desperately to keep on track with college work: he was eventually kicked out because he was too far behind. He's also had to take on the role of carer for his father, who needed help around the house. Through all of that, we've done our best to stick with him and, more surprisingly, he has stuck with us.

Troy has also become part of our worshipping community and made a commitment to faith, along with his girlfriend. This September he joined our team in Alway as a Youth Work Apprentice by living in our Lab community house, becoming committed to serving the local community and gaining youth work skills and experience. One of the most inspiring, emotional experiences for me was interviewing Troy for the apprenticeship place. He was so passionate about his community, and determined to help, that there was no way our interview panel could turn him down.

When we asked Troy what being part of The Lab community meant to him, this is what he wrote:

The Lab has taught me to calm down and make the most of this short-lived life… The Lab has helped me out a lot, so it's awesome for me to help give other young people the options and advice that were given to me by the very people I now work with.

Lessons we've learned along the way

Here are five lessons we've learned from our experience of mission among young adults. Some have been learned the hard way, from failed attempts and frustrating ongoing struggles. Others are ideas that have come naturally to us as we've followed God's call, but that we've found to be key to our ministry's success.

Don't start with sung worship

When The Lab began, we started straight away by organising a worship gathering or service on a Sunday evening. This was very effective at drawing together a group of Christian young adults who could form our core group to get the ministry started, but also had major drawbacks. It took a huge amount of patience and effort to shift our mindsets away from planning worship in a style that we liked and enjoyed, to actively praying and seeking to engage with young adults who were outside the reach of the church.

We were incredibly blessed because God drew a group of Christian students to join us who had travelled into the city from outside and were struggling to find a church community where they could settle. Today, there are so many different thriving churches with student ministries in Newport that I think our situation would be difficult to replicate. Many churches are really effective at supporting, discipling and providing worship opportunities for already-Christian students, but there is a great need for new ministries that are willing to take risks in engaging with non-Christian young adults and their culture. In order to do this, I think we need to start in a different place.

When Jesus called his first disciples (Luke 5), he went out to where they already were, in order to find them. He would have known that there were many young fishermen who went about their family trade every day on the shores of the sea of Galilee. Unlike many other religious leaders of his time, he didn't wait for followers to gather around him. He knew the people God was calling him to reach, so he met them where they were. When it comes to mission with young adults, the lesson I've learned is to begin where young adults already are and engage with them there, rather than expecting them to come to our church events and gatherings.

Loving community is vital for individual discipleship

When The Lab began, I assumed that the best way to disciple young adults was to think about each of them individually. One of the things I've learned over the last few years is that effective discipleship is a community process. The most effective way to disciple individual young adults is to create a communal culture where they feel cared for, supported and sometimes challenged by each other. In her research into fresh expressions of church among young adults, Beth Keith found that community is a key value within young adult fresh expressions, writing, 'The term "family" was used frequently, particularly in reference to church as family, both for those from broken family backgrounds, or a family away from home for those having recently moved away from their parents' home for university or jobs' (*Authentic Faith*, Fresh Expressions, 2013).

This learning was cemented for me when we tried to adapt and develop our midweek activities. When we shifted away from having a weekly community meal and, instead, held small groups based mostly on Bible study, we were surprised to find that this had a negative effect on the level of community in The Lab and on people's individual discipleship. It became much harder to ensure that everyone was supported pastorally, because there was less opportunity for informal conversation rather than formal theological discussion. Even though there was more discussion about discipleship taking place, we saw less of the fruit of discipleship in our community life.

Authenticity is more important than clarity

Another lesson we've learned, which follows on from the importance of community, is that most young adults value authenticity and honesty much more than big events or programmes. This generation of young adults has grown up surrounded by so many advertising messages, and so many stories of corporate greed and corruption, that many have an innate suspicion of hierarchy, structure and marketing. They know that there's no such thing as a free lunch and, if something seems too good to be true, it probably is.

The same applies to the way in which we share our beliefs. Young adults are not interested in a version of the gospel that leaves no room for questions or doubts. Instead, more and more young adults are being drawn towards leaders and communities who aren't afraid to be honest about their struggles, failures and imperfections.

Change is the only constant

Another of Beth Keith's insights is that young adult communities go through changes and transitions at breakneck pace. We've experienced huge changes when key community members have moved on because they've graduated or have found work elsewhere. This means that, in the space of a couple of months, The Lab might be made up of an entirely different group of young adults. These changes in personnel might not be caused by a geographical move, either. Often, someone might start working in the evenings or at the weekend and we might not see them for several months. Those in our community who are still studying at university regularly drop in and out of contact when they have assignments to complete or exams to revise for.

We've had to learn quickly and adapt to changes that come our way, regularly altering shape and drawing new people into leadership. If an activity looks as if it's stagnating, we are not afraid to put a stop to it and try something else.

For a couple of years, we really struggled to form a leadership team made up of young adults who would help make decisions, organise events and lead worship gatherings. It was a struggle because there was such a high turnover of people. Then we realised that we could be much more flexible if we held open leadership meetings. This way, the people who were available and willing at that time would come. We always had enough people to discuss and make plans, even when some of our key people were out of action.

Challenge young people to discover God's mission

Our most energising and exciting, as well as toughest, task over the last seven years has been challenging young adults to engage in God's mission by loving, serving and sharing the good news with others. Through our apprenticeship scheme, we've seen lots of young adults empowered to think missionally and grow in leadership, with many choosing to stay for several years and some developing into different forms of Christian ministry afterwards.

Not long after The Lab started, I was challenged to ask myself the question: what difference would it make if our ministry no longer existed? Would anyone miss us? Would the local community be any worse off, or even better off, without us? It was these questions that spurred me on to challenge our whole community to engage in loving and serving others. Over time, our mission initiatives and projects have become the heart of what we do as a community, providing an extra edge to our worship, prayer and discipleship.

A key part of Jesus' strategy for developing his disciples was to commission them and send them out. In Luke 9:2, only four chapters after he calls the first disciples, he sends out the Twelve 'to proclaim the kingdom of God and to heal those who were ill'. Then, a chapter later, he sends out another 72 (Luke 10:1). It is clear that Jesus didn't see this commissioning as the end of his disciples' learning. They didn't have to wait to graduate to be sent out; it was an important part of their formation as disciples to do themselves what they had seen Jesus doing already.

My big challenge as a leader is to marry up the gifts of the young adults who join us with the needs of the local communities with which we're involved. Every young adult brings a different personality, gifts and talents, so it's important to find roles that fit each person. This way, serving in mission will energise rather than drain them.

Engaging in mission with young adults in your context

Find out where the young adults are

Before doing anything, take time to explore and understand the young adult culture around you. What different friendship groups exist among young adults in your context? Whether you live in a town, city or rural village, these questions are always important. Finally, where do the young adults around you spend their time?

Here are some suggestions of common places:

- Coffee shops
- Bars, pubs and clubs

- Societies and clubs based on hobbies or interests
- Sports teams

If you're looking to engage with students, many of them will spend the majority of their time on the university campus. What social spaces exist there? Does the Student Union run a café or bar? What societies are proving popular among students? Is there a university chaplain who could be a friend or partner in your ministry?

Once you have an idea of the places where young adults are hanging out and the things they are interested in, you can formulate some ideas for how to build initial relationships with them. This might be as simple as becoming a regular at a coffee shop, or it could mean putting on a series of social events yourself.

Build family around the table

When you have made some natural connections with young adults in your community, the next step is to try to deepen the sense of community and extended family, which many young adults are searching for. We have found that the best way to do this is around the dinner table, with plenty of wholesome food and lots of banter and conversation. It's important to invite the young adults to play a part in hosting and even cooking the meals, as this will help a supportive community to develop.

Only then, once young adults are part of a supportive, loving community where they feel safe, will they be able and willing to open up to questions about faith, spirituality and discipleship.

Develop young adults as apprentices

Once a supportive community is taking shape, you can begin to think about the most appropriate way to share faith with the young adults you are getting to know. We've found that the most successful way to equip young adults for lifelong discipleship is to begin apprenticing them early on, before they've even made a commitment to faith. Get them engaged in social justice issues, find ways together to serve those who are less fortunate and begin to explore together what it means to live in the way of Jesus. When they are challenged with a different, more fulfilled way of living, many young adults will want to get to know the God who has inspired it.

7

Wide Open

Kay Morgan-Gurr is a children's evangelist and disability adviser. With her husband Steve, she runs Children Worldwide, a network of independent children's workers serving the church among children and families. She has a wealth of experience in working with young people with additional needs.

Paula Smith helps to run a holiday aimed at children and young people with additional needs. The residential, called Wide Open, aims to connect young people in a Christian context, making the environment and spiritual content as open and accessible as possible, so that all can take part.

Wide Open accepts young people aged 14–19 and caters specifically for the additional needs that each participant might have.

Working with young people with additional needs

Kay writes:

Let me introduce you to Bella. She is a teenager with attitude —and cerebral palsy. Her hair is pink, she enjoys discussions on reincarnation, is amused by our pleas over her use of certain words and phrases and has successfully smuggled a huge bottle of vodka on to a camp we were running (although we did find it within twelve hours of her arrival). We had to do all our communication slowly and via her 'talker'. Bella blows every preconception you could have about working with young people who have additional needs. In short, she is just like many other teenagers.

There are lots of teenagers and pre-teens in our youth work for whom we have to think differently about how to approach them. Take two more of my friends as examples. Harry has Down's syndrome and autism. He hangs around the back of the youth programme, walking up and down constantly. The walking is his way of coping. When he can't cope, he shakes the stuffed rabbit he always carries. He can cope when there is order and when someone is helping him understand what is going on. He likes to know what is happening before he arrives, and appreciates time on his own outside the programme, especially when there is bustle and noise. He finds it difficult to engage with the teaching unless someone takes the time to adapt it for him.

Philip is 15 but thinks like an eight-year-old and is also dyslexic. He is very caring and loves to help out where he can. He's able to hold his own in the youth group but struggles to follow some of the teaching, especially when so much of it relies on being able to read. He loves the noise of worship but finds it difficult to follow lyrics or even understand what they mean at times. He finds it impossible to read words displayed on a screen with moving backgrounds. His favourite times are when leaders chat to him about what has been taught, while he is helping to tidy things up. It's in those times that the leaders can find ways to support him better. For example, they found out that Philip reads more easily when words are printed on cream paper with a larger font, so they started to reproduce song words and readings in that format for each session.

Both these boys have real difficulty in accessing things that normally happen in a youth group setting, but their leaders are open to supporting them. Those leaders have a vision for them and their journey with God.

'Yes' is possibly the most important word we can use in the area of additional needs—'yes' to accepting these young people into our programmes; 'yes' to finding alternative ways to worship and teach; in short, 'yes' to inclusion and belonging. There is a distinct difference between inclusion and belonging. You can experience inclusion without feeling as if you belong. We need both.

The way we do youth work is often not helpful to young people who have an additional need. It tends to be fast-moving, loud and without a regular routine. We go to places and do activities that some young people cannot access, and we use methods of communicating our message that many cannot connect with. For the majority in our groups, these methods and activities are exciting and good, but, for the one in five of our young people who have additional needs, they can be unhelpful, disorientating and exclusive.

Facilitating inclusion and belonging for some of our older

children and teenagers is not easy. It takes planning, time and extra volunteers. It takes a different way of thinking. The first step to successful inclusion and belonging is to have a vision for it. These youngsters are not a problem to be solved or people who stand between us and the way we would rather do things. They are, like any other person in your youth work, young people with the ability to love and respond to God, to be filled with the Spirit and to have a vibrant relationship with him. We may not always understand how they connect with God, but they do.

We often expect 'inclusion' to mean having all the young people together all of the time, whereas inclusion or belonging can mean offering time alone, out of the programme, when space is needed, or providing a few minutes in which a simple summary of teaching is given.

Making our youth work accessible for those with additional needs means that our youth work will be accessible to all who attend. You may not have young people with any obvious additional needs, as many of those needs are hidden, so bear this in mind too. Think about these things:

- How would you feel about a 15-year-old who is on the autistic spectrum having a hand-held games console with them? Would you take it away or recognise that it may be a tool that helps them engage with the activities going on around them?
- How do you facilitate worship and Bible reading? Are songs and reading accessible to all, or do you need to find alternative formats?
- Are your activities accessible—not just physically, but also for those with sensory problems and for those with learning disabilities?

- How would a young person who is deaf or blind cope with your activities?
- What about young people associated with your youth work who have illnesses that prevent them coming to church, such as ME or another form of severe or chronic illness? How do you help them to feel included and loved? Have you ever thought of Skyping your youth meetings? Do you continue to invite these young people to events even though they won't be able to attend? I know many in this position who value being invited even though they can't go.
- How about auditing all of your youth work and checking it for accessibility? You may not have anyone with some of the more specific needs, but it's good to have a plan in place for when you do.

Wide Open

Paula writes:

Back in 2003, a small group of women (of whom I was one), all with some experience of learning disability and a desire to help young people with such difficulties 'connect' with God, met to consider the possibility of a holiday, under the auspices of Scripture Union, aimed specifically at the 13–19 age range.

Our group was aware that there were young people who were able (in most cases) to engage physically in the activities of a holiday but struggled to connect with the social, emotional and spiritual aspects. Due to their learning disability, they were sometimes daunted by too much choice, a fast pace, lots of people and too much noise.

They needed something on a smaller scale, in a venue that

was easier to navigate than a boarding school or activity centre (where such events are often located), and, importantly, with Bible teaching delivered in an accessible manner—in other words, age-appropriate but simplified.

The result of this discussion was the Wide Open holiday, which has been running now for ten years at the Great Wood site in Somerset. The holiday caters for approximately 20 teenagers, with a high ratio of helpers offering support and guidance. The young people spend four nights away.

The same, but more accessible

The activities during the holiday are the same as many others—opportunities to cook, play games, make craft, walk, swim and make music—but many of them take place in small groups rather than having the whole group together. Often, young people with additional learning needs find it difficult to be in a large group, so some of our activities are run in groups of about six, with lots of adult support and supervision. This is particularly key in the more overtly spiritual times, when Bible stories and teaching can be opened in the most appropriate way for the young people in each small group.

Bible discovery is delivered interactively, usually focusing on stories in the New Testament. In our planning we spend time considering the key truths that we want to get across, asking ourselves, 'What is the one main point that comes out of a specific story?' We then try to reinforce that teaching in a variety of ways, but we try never to overcomplicate the message. We seek to involve young people in the telling of the story, through drama or creating sound effects and with a variety of visual aids. Visual impact is important as it helps immerse young people in what they're going to discover. We decorate the room we are using, to set the scene.

After each day's Bible teaching, we offer each young person an object of reference—something to take away to help them remember the main theme of the meeting. Memory aids are useful with all young people, but a visual reminder of what they have discovered helps many young people with additional needs to connect with God and keep reflecting on their experience, long after the session has finished. Similarly, we teach a short memory verse (one for the whole holiday). The young people have great fun memorising it and, through the verse, they are given another hook on which to hang the teaching.

On the final morning, parents are invited to a short presentation, where we give a summary of the Bible teaching and an idea of the various activities we have done during the week. This is important for those youngsters for whom communication is difficult, and it has proved valuable to parents when they want to help their child recall the holiday. Every young person is offered a CD of photos in order to aid conversation about the week once they are back home with their families.

Jesus knows me by name

This summer, our teaching theme was 'Jesus knows me by name'. The young people were encouraged to learn an adapted version of Psalm 139:1: 'God sees me and knows me'. Our stories focused on four people whom Jesus met and knew by name. Activities were tailored to the Bible teaching: young people made name plaques out of clay, and we iced cakes on the day we heard about Zacchaeus, thinking about Jesus choosing to go to his house for a meal.

After the holiday, one parent contacted me to say how well her son had connected with this theme. She wanted to use the same ideas to help those with additional needs to connect with the teaching at her church holiday club.

One young man with Down's syndrome has been coming to the holiday for five or six years. He was introduced to Wide Open by a friend (also with Down's syndrome) whose family are Christians. One year, towards the end of the holiday, when everyone was asked, 'What has been the best part of the holiday?' he answered, 'Jesus is in my heart.' He and his family now attend his friend's church.

Another young man has been baptised in recent months and, despite a severe speech defect, wanted to tell us about it while he was at this year's holiday. With the aid of a PowerPoint presentation put together by his family, he shared his story. Wide Open had obviously helped him to get to know Jesus, and he quoted one of the memory verses he had learned at the holiday a few years ago.

One girl, whose ability it could be easy to underestimate, came alive during worship times and really enjoyed music. She loved to dance, raising her hands and joining in action songs. One evening, she wanted to sit quietly after our meeting. I went over to pray with her and together we simply thanked Jesus for his love and forgiveness. Later that evening, after the excitement of a special meal and a talent show, she came over to me, gave me a hug and said, 'Thank you' as she put her hands together in a gesture of prayer.

Practical considerations

We have found it important and reassuring for many of the young people to have a timetable that they can refer to each day, so that they know what will be happening and in what order. This helps those who need to know the day's events (for example, those on the autistic spectrum). They know in advance when activities are ending and new ones beginning. Having this timetable reduces anxiety, and its visual nature means that the young people don't need to read to understand what is happening. The only difficulty it presents is that bad weather or other circumstances sometimes force us to make last-minute changes to our planned schedule.

Having a site with good access and facilities is also key. The Scripture Union site at Great Wood in Somerset is an 'outdoor' venue, not a boarding school or residential centre. With its ensuite log cabins set around a large, flat, central grassed area, it is ideal for those with mobility issues, as it has none of the tight corners or narrow corridors of schools and centres. The cabins also help to accommodate the smaller groups needed for young people with additional learning needs.

The high ratio of leaders to young people is another important consideration. Many young people with additional needs require more help emotionally and socially, as well as physically. Having a good adult-to-participant ratio helps young people to become active and flourishing members of the community, removing the risk of isolation that is caused by many additional needs. Trying something new or meeting people for the first time can be quite scary, so no one is made to join in, but everyone is encouraged to try.

Longer-term impact

We have seen young people grow in confidence and increase their level of independence in their personal care, life skills and choice-making. One girl had never washed her own hair; another had not ridden a bike; some had not made a sandwich for themselves. Parents have commented with gratitude about these developments. Although these things do not represent our main aim in running the holiday, they are an encouraging side-effect of the level of support and the tailoring of activities to the young people's needs.

Over the years, I have met families who've told me how important it has been for their child with additional needs to go on their own residential event, catering for their particular needs, just as their siblings have been able to do.

The holiday has also provided an opportunity for two young people, after they grew too old to come as campers, to return in a junior leader role. They undertook simple specific tasks each day, helping with the practical running of the holiday. They may not have had the opportunity to do this in another setting, and it helped their development and independence.

Going forward

Looking into the future, I think it is important not to assume that we want a bigger holiday. It would require more adult help and would lead to a group size that would be disconcerting or distressing for many of the young people. Instead, we're considering replicating Wide Open elsewhere, to provide chances for more young people to become part of a temporary Christian community that caters for their needs and helps them meet God.

Through the Roof

Through the Roof is a Christian disability charity that, for the past six years, has run a family holiday for a small number of families affected by autism. Many such families tell us that church 'doesn't work' for their autistic young people, who find the noise, the crowded rooms and the many words in the service too much to cope with. In the environment of this specialised holiday, each family is given a one-to-one helper for their autistic child. Activities are planned carefully, just as they are at Wide Open. Autistic children often find it more comfortable to do things in their own space, not necessarily in a group with others.

The Bible teaching (delivered in a mixed group of those with autism and their siblings) is, again, very interactive. A short, simple story backed up by a choice of activities reinforcing the main teaching point—questions to answer, worksheets and things to make—allows an autistic young person the chance to respond in a way that is best for them.

We sometimes hold a simple Communion service for the whole family during the holiday. At the service, we set up tables with bread and grape juice, each table labelled with a family's name. After a simple explanation of Jesus' last meal with his twelve special friends, each family shares the food on their table as they remember Jesus. One family told us that this was particularly good for them, as their daughter had never been able to sit in church and join in, so they had all been prevented from taking part in Holy Communion. The family were moved and delighted to be able to do this together in an environment where their daughter felt 'safe'.

Welcoming young people with additional needs in your context

- Remember that we are all individuals and respond to God differently.
- Draw out one main teaching point from a Bible passage and reinforce it in a variety of ways.
- Give lots of options in terms of follow-up activities once your main teaching point has been conveyed, but give guidance to those who struggle with choice.

- Don't assess a person just by what the eye can see. We are all like icebergs: there's a lot below the surface.
- Try doing things differently sometimes, even if it is for the benefit of only one person.
- At the beginning of a session, set out an outline of what is going to happen or put up a timetable.
- Keep things simple.

To me, 1 Corinthians 1:18–29 puts into perspective God's heart for those with additional needs:

God purposely chose what the world considers nonsense in order to shame the wise, and he chose what the world considers weak in order to shame the powerful. He chose what the world looks down on and despises, and thinks is nothing, in order to destroy what the world thinks is important. This means that no one can boast in God's presence (vv. 27–29, GNB).

8

Hope MK

*Ricky Rew is youth pastor at
Spurgeon's Baptist Church
in Bletchley, Milton Keynes.
Together with Pat Kerr,
youth leader at St Mary's
Bletchley, and Rosie Harriett
from Bridgebuilder Trust, he
set up Hope MK, an event
to help young people reach
out to their local community,
make a difference and tell
people about Jesus. They
embarked on a year-long
process to prepare for the
week of activities and
outreach, and, despite ups
and downs, facilitated a great
week of mission, growth and
community involvement.*

Beyond Belief

Over recent years, there had been a growing sense among church leaders, youth workers and organisations that the Lord was moving in exciting ways across Milton Keynes, specifically in relation to young people. Churches and organisations were doing great work with young Christians and seeing their investment bear fruit. Young people were excited about their relationship with Jesus and enthusiastic about his call on their lives to 'go and make disciples'. At a time when youngsters were being increasingly demonised in the media and by politicians, young Christians were smashing those stereotypes apart, and, more excitingly, wanting to enable their peers to do the same. With a desire to seize the opportunity and make best use of the momentum, in November 2012 a group of leaders got together to dream about how we could impact the city by empowering young people to do local mission and encouraging churches to work together more closely to support and resource them.

One church from Milton Keynes had joined a ten-day residential mission in Cambridge called Beyond Belief a few years earlier. Their youth leader gave an overview of what it involved and how it worked, and, more importantly, shared stories of the mission's impact on the faith of those who took part. The young people grew in faith during the mission as they saw God at work and realised he could use them to bless others. In the months that followed, their faith continued to grow as they were able to relate what they read in scripture to their own experiences. The mission week became a foundation from which there was continued growth. It was a compelling example of young people being transformed through mission, and we agreed to use the model of Beyond

Belief as a starting point for our plans, forming a core team to explore the idea of something similar for Milton Keynes.

From there, Hope MK was born with a vision to enable young Christians to bless and serve the communities of Milton Keynes with God's love and grace, by teaching and equipping them to put their faith into practice and empowering them to engage in mission in their own city. We determined that it would be a five-day mission for young people (Year 7 and older), serving on projects running across the city, blessing communities in practical ways and engaging in conversational evangelism. The mission would culminate in a big evangelistic event, to which we would invite young people as we served.

Our intention was for everyone to spend the mornings together in one place for a time of team-building, teaching, worship and prayer. After lunch (Monday to Thursday), they would head out across the city to serve on their projects before coming back together for dinner and a time to reflect, share their experiences and pray together. On Friday afternoon we would send the teams out with evangelistic challenges to undertake instead of working on their projects, returning for dinner before heading to the big gig.

With the vision discerned, and having worked out how to achieve it, we had the challenge of making it all happen.

Moving forward in Milton Keynes

The first phase of the initiative was to share the vision with churches in Milton Keynes and encourage them to get involved. With over 140 churches across the city, that was never going to be easy. We had a series of face-to-face meetings with church leaders and youth leaders we knew, explaining the vision and asking them to get involved and to extend the invitation to their church and their network of contacts. But there's a limit to the amount of time available for that approach (and to the amount of coffee we can drink). We arranged a meeting and invited as many church leaders and youth leaders as we could contact to join us to hear about the vision for Hope MK. In April 2013, we were joined by representatives of more than 30 churches of different sizes, traditions and denominations. By the end of the meeting, there was overwhelming agreement that Hope MK was long overdue, that the approach we'd planned and outlined would work and that we would achieve it together in partnership.

As we presented, discussed, listened and prayed, Psalm 133 came to mind, where David expresses how great it is when God's people live together in harmony and unity because it is there that God commands his blessing. When God's people set aside differences and focus on what we have in common, God pours out his blessing like an anointing with expensive oil. We left the meeting with a spring in our step and those words of scripture in our hearts, trusting for the blessing to be poured out.

We tasked the leaders present to return to their churches to share the vision and get involved. There were five ways we were encouraging their involvement:

- **Prayer:** we were trusting God to honour the vision he'd given, but we needed prayer every step of the way.
- **Projects:** we needed churches (and groups of churches) to run social action projects for the week on which the young people would serve.
- **People:** we required adults for project leadership and in supporting roles (catering, transport and so on).

- **Sponsorship:** with no funding, we relied on churches and individuals giving financially to support the initiative through donations, sponsoring elements, fundraising and so on.
- **Young people:** we needed churches to encourage their young people to commit to joining us.

We asked churches to organise and lead social action and community-building projects on which the young people would serve, encouraging them to meet a need in their local community, working together with other local churches and organisations wherever possible. There were some great examples of partnership working, but most projects were run by individual churches. As well as meeting a local need, we stipulated that projects must present opportunities for the young people to engage in conversational evangelism. It was important to make this clear when discussing any partnership with non-Christian community organisations, as, for some organisations, the evangelistic intent would mean that they were unable to work with us.

Alongside the efforts to get churches involved, we were visiting youth events and church services to share the vision among young people themselves. There was a brilliant response, with young people getting excited about the challenge and the opportunity, but, as any youth leader will tell you, converting that enthusiasm into any kind of commitment is a long and difficult process. There was a limit to what we could do, and we were reliant on individual churches and youth leaders to get their young people to sign up. We were fully aware that the commitment we were seeking was huge. We were asking young people to give up their half-term break, step into the unknown for five long days, and pay for the privilege too (a registration fee to cover some of the costs). But having heard about the impact of the Cambridge mission on the young people who took part, we were confident that the time and effort they invested would be rewarded.

As Hope MK developed, the scariest issue to address was that of funding. There would be certain fixed costs and many variable costs (dependent on the number of young people and adult volunteers who signed up), but there wasn't any money initially. We were completely reliant on churches, organisations and individuals being prepared to invest in the initiative, and young people being prepared to pay the registration fee. We had some early donations, which were very encouraging, many churches promised financial support (and all but one fulfilled their promise) and we had some very generous donations from individuals. We also undertook one small fundraising event to raise a little extra money. The total central costs were £10,346 and the total income was £10,455 (33 per cent registration fees, 55 per cent donations from churches and organisations, seven per cent donations from individuals and five per cent through fundraising). Some people have suggested that this was down to experienced budget management and great planning, but we know that it was entirely due to God's provision and blessings.

All the plans came together in a truly beautiful week, and God blessed it all. We divided the young people into eleven teams, each with eight to twelve young people. Here's a brief overview of the projects that ran each afternoon from Monday to Thursday.

• Drop and play: pop-up play sessions at local parks and youth centres.

- Late lunch: providing lunch and activities for children from deprived families.
- Coffee Hall community clean-up: mural painting on a disused church and litter-picking around the Coffee Hall estate.
- Free car wash: exactly as the name suggests, but with refreshments and conversation available.
- Pop-up footie cage: mobile mini-football arena for four-man tournaments.
- Family drop-in centre: arts, crafts and activities for all ages.
- Youth café: video games, crafts and activities for young people.
- Residential care home roadshow: visiting homes with skits, songs and smiles.
- Creative gardening: landscaping and maintaining a public garden outside a large central church.
- Creative evangelism: a range of activities to challenge the team and bless the people they met.
- Listening post: mobile sofas and a team with sweets and a listening ear.

At the end of each day, we spent time together sharing stories, reflecting on what had happened, discussing what we'd learned, giving thanks and praying about the challenges we would face the next day. It was such an encouraging time; even if a team felt they'd had a tough day, to hear about God at work through others was a real boost to everyone.

On the final afternoon, the teams were taken further out of their comfort zones when they were presented with evangelistic challenges to undertake and provided with appropriate resources. Even the team leaders didn't know what they would be doing.

The challenges included:

- Free parking: hanging around car park meters and offering to pay for the first hour's parking for shoppers.
- Trade-up: attempting to trade items of little value for items of greater value, with the aim of giving away whatever they had at the end in order to bless someone.
- Free doughnuts: giving away doughnuts with a smile and engaging people in conversation.
- Positive post-its: writing positive messages on post-it notes and sticking them around town, or, if feeling brave, handing them to someone personally.
- Your choice: team members were given £25 with no instructions other than to use it to bless people and engage them in conversation.
- Free lollipops: giving away lollipops with a smile and engaging people in conversation.
- Bus rides and lollipops: travelling around on buses, giving away lollipops and engaging people in conversation.

As the week progressed, we were repeatedly delighted, surprised and amazed by the stories we were hearing from the teams. It was an absolute joy to see young people and adult volunteers alike growing in confidence. Most of the projects and activities were really simple ideas, but they afforded incredible opportunities to engage with people. Some projects and activities were fun and activity-based, while others were more challenging and offered opportunities to engage on a deeper level. Some conversations naturally led to team members offering to pray with or for the individuals, and all offers were accepted. We also gave each young person and adult volunteer a copy of the New Testament at the start of the week and encouraged them to ask God to prompt them about who to give it to.

To sum up in a single sentence, 108 young people stepped out in faith, investing 5400 hours through eleven social action and community-building projects, engaging with over 1500 Milton Keynes residents and visitors, supported by 22 churches and four Christian organisations in partnership with three national and 15 local organisations.

But it's not just about numbers. What has been the lasting impact of Hope MK?

A big impact

We were completely blown away by what happened through Hope MK. We worked on it for over a year and arrived at the start utterly exhausted, but very quickly saw that all the hard work had been worthwhile. At times during the week, we were moved to tears, and, as we continue to reflect on what was achieved, those tears are not far away. We are still hearing stories about how people were positively affected by everything that happened during Hope MK; some are incredibly powerful and others very simple but no less important.

Impact on those we served

The 'Late lunch' project provided a hot meal for children from deprived families who are entitled to free school meals but whose families struggle to feed them properly during school holidays. The team were disappointed by the fact that they were joined by only eight or ten children each day, having planned to cater for 30, but the children who attended didn't just receive a free hot meal; they also had one-to-one attention from the team members (adults and young people). The play sessions after lunch became the highlight for the children. Lunch was nice, but to have such focused attention for over an hour was new for many of them. At the end of the sessions, the children didn't want to leave because they'd had so much fun. The actions and attitudes of the project team were a practical expression of the love of God in action.

The 'Drop and play' project spent two afternoons at a local skatepark, trying to engage with and get to know the local skateboarders. Attempting to break into such a well-established and close-knit group was never going to be easy, but the team built a great rapport with the skaters, inviting them to play games and chat. Before long, the skaters were allowing some of the team members to borrow their skateboards and join in on the skatepark.

We estimate that, through the week, 1500 people of all ages across Milton Keynes had a positive engagement with Christians and more than 30 people were willing to receive prayer. Some have let us know that those prayers have been answered. Here's one example from a project leader:

> Early in the week, the creative evangelism team met a lady and asked if there was anything she'd like them to pray for; she said she desperately needed a coat. They prayed, she thanked them, and they went on their way.
>
> On Friday the same lady, with a beaming face, approached another team (recognising their blue hoodies) and wanted to say thank you. God had answered that prayer and she was wearing her new coat.

Without doubt, the greatest impact came through one of our evangelistic challenges, when, through a series of trades, one team on the trade-up challenge swapped their bottle of bubbles for a wedding dress. (You can read the full incredible story on our website: www.hopemk.com/news/greater.)

Impact on those reached through the evangelistic gig

Through the week, the project teams were giving away free tickets to young people aged 11–17, inviting them to join us for the evangelistic event on Friday evening. In addition to the 100-plus Hope MK young people, there were approximately 50 young people from church youth groups and 100 young people who had no church connection at all. The event was to be a celebration of the hard work the teams had invested through the week, including a time of worship, giving thanks to God for all he'd done. It also included some Christian performers who talked about how their faith informs their work, and concluded with the self-confessed 'former scumbag' (now evangelist) Gram Seed sharing his life story and explaining how God transformed him.

Gram encouraged everyone present to respond to God's free gift of forgiveness through Jesus. As we ended the evening in worship, 14 young people talked with the ministry team and received prayer, and nine young people responded and received Jesus as their Lord and Saviour. They were given a Bible and put in touch with a local church.

In the week after Hope MK, we heard of one lad who wanted to respond to what Gram Seed shared but had to leave early. He was so compelled to respond, however, that he turned up at a church two days later and committed his life to the Lord.

Many of the young people who attended that night will have heard the gospel for the first time and were challenged to reconnect with a God who loves them passionately. Who knows when those seeds may bear fruit?

Impact on those who served

At the start of the week, we saw nervous and timid young people arriving at the venue wondering what on earth they'd let themselves in for. Through the week, we saw their confidence increase and their faith deepen as they saw God at work through them and around them, and heard similar stories shared by their friends. Five of the young people who served for the week gave their lives to Jesus during the morning teaching sessions. The best way to explain the impact it had on the young people and the adult volunteers is to use their own words.

Here are some comments from young people:

It was a life-changing experience for me.

I used to think that God's miracles were just for thousands of years ago, but now I've seen some for myself.

At Hope MK I stepped out of my comfort zone and realised that God was already there!

I cried as I got in the car to head home. I was having flashbacks every second showing me what an amazing opportunity I'd had, and I couldn't believe it was over. I learnt so much and gave my life to the Lord along the way. I had so much fun that I can't express it. I can't wait until next year. My hoodie is ironed and ready to go!

And from some adult volunteers:

I love our parishioners, but structural church life in Milton Keynes isn't easy. Through Hope MK, I've caught a vision of why God wants me here.

It was really heart-warming to see young people of so many churches befriending each other, praying for each other, and working together to serve the wider community.

Impact on the church in Milton Keynes

It was an absolute joy to see so many churches of different sizes and denominations working well together. There were one or two conversations about differences in our theology, but they were among the adults. The young people were a beautiful demonstration of the church that Jesus prayed for in John 17—sent out into the world, as one, brought to complete unity so that the world may believe. Just about every adult commented on the overwhelming sense of unity through the week. One said, 'I was touched almost to tears a number of times by the sense of love and unity in the Spirit that was present among us. It felt almost like finding long-lost brothers and sisters.' Many prejudices were shattered that week as we came to see through the stereotypes and into the lives of Christians of other traditions and denominations.

There are more than 140 churches in Milton Keynes, but for that week in October 2013 there was just one Church, and we saw it work in a way that has never before been seen in the city. The blessing that we'd been promised from Psalm 133 at our first formal meeting was poured out extravagantly and unmistakably.

The church in Milton Keynes has seen what happens when Christians of all ages and denominations work together, leaving the comfort of their buildings behind to serve their local communities, with no agenda other than to bless people with God's love and talk about why they're doing it. People at all stages of faith have stepped out into the unknown and have 'done evangelism' and the resounding message is that they survived, they enjoyed it and God used them.

We've seen faith deepened, confidence increased and we've seen God at work outside our church buildings. Then we've seen those who were involved sharing their experiences with anyone who will listen. What an impact!

Revd Chris Duffett, an evangelist with the Light Project, says, 'Hope MK has given me a hunch about the future of the Church in the UK.'

For more stories, take a look at our website, which is full of photos, comments and testimonies of the week (visit http://hopemk.com).

Where next?

You probably have a very rosy view of Hope MK and are assuming that the process was peaceful and straightforward, but don't be fooled. We certainly didn't get everything right, and it wasn't easy. In fact, the preparation was so all-consuming that, a week before we were due to start, we were absolutely adamant that it would be a one-off event. But by the end of the week it was clear that this was just the beginning of an important and necessary journey—so we're doing it all again.

One message came across loud and clear during our teaching times: mission is a lifestyle to be lived, not a week to be experienced. The call on our lives to 'go and make disciples' cannot be limited to one week each year, so the challenge to the churches and youth groups is to ensure that they encourage each other to live out an ongoing life of mission in word and deed. We will be playing our part, too. We are planning a number of small-scale activities that will build on the experiences of Hope MK—challenges that will require just a couple of hours of people's time and much less organisation.

We recognise that the community that developed through Hope MK needs to be nurtured, too, and it's important for us to continue to hear stories of how God is at work through these young people. There are plans for a couple of Hope MK youth services this year, which will offer a chance for the team to gather to worship and pray together, and for teaching and equipping. There will also be a training day for project leaders and young leaders, to ensure that they're properly equipped as well.

During the week, some of the leaders felt that God was challenging them about what Hope MK would look like in three years' and 20 years' time, so we are faithfully following where God leads. We're not set on one particular model, and we're not even convinced that the particular 'youth mission' focus will remain, but it really feels as if there's more going on, and we're excited about what that might be.

Setting up local community action projects in your context

We know that we made mistakes along the way, but we learned some valuable lessons too.

- Don't get carried away by the enthusiasm of others. This is a lesson we almost learned the hard way. Having developed the practical plan for Hope MK as a small team, when we shared it with others in a larger setting they were really excited. They politely suggested that we were thinking too small, that our chosen venue would limit the scope of the initiative and that we needed to double our estimate of the number of young people who would be involved. We were really encouraged by their enthusiasm, advice and promises of support. As a result, we nearly spent £2000 to secure a venue that would have been too big and impractical. Thankfully, after a great deal of discussion and prayer, we went with our original plan. The venue was almost perfect and the number of young people we had anticipated was almost spot-on too.

- Don't count on every promise being fulfilled. Make your plans flexible enough to cope with changes. It is easier for churches to support financially than to support with human resources. In our experience, 95 per cent of the promises of financial support were fulfilled, but fewer than 50 per cent of the promises to run projects or provide young people and adult volunteers were kept.

- Keep the planning and development team small (three to five people). Organising anything by committee is a very difficult process, and the more successful you are at getting churches and organisations involved, the greater the risk that the committee will become unmanageable and impotent. We made nearly all the key decisions in the small core team but communicated them to the wider stakeholders. We used two sub-teams to organise specific aspects of the event (the Friday night gig being the best example) but had regular meetings to ensure that the progress being made was in line with the vision that had been expressed.

- Getting churches to buy into the agenda of another organisation and support somebody else's vision has always proved difficult. Early on, we were asked, 'How is Hope MK going to be any more successful than what we've done before?' We think the main difference is that, while the initiative was limited (to the October half-term) and prescriptive (four days of mission, with mornings spent on team-building and teaching, and afternoons on projects), many of the projects had a longer-term potential and impact. Local churches knew their communities far better than we did and were more aware of local needs. We encouraged churches to consider the needs in their local community and how best to meet them, then to develop a project that did just that, working with other organisations if appropriate. Some churches had projects in mind long before Hope MK, but had been unable to run them due to a lack of willing volunteers. They were able to engage a team of young people from Hope MK and run the project for a week. So the churches were still able to serve their own local agenda by meeting the needs of their community, if they wished to. (It's worth noting that five of the eleven projects served 'other' communities.)

- Some individuals are reluctant to get on board with something new. Some churches need to know that a vision is achievable before signing up, and some individuals need to see what an event will look like before they feel comfortable signing up (or allowing their children to do so). Be content simply to accept that, and don't fret about it. We invested lots of time chasing people, trying to convince them. We don't mean to offend anyone, but we found the following stereotypes to be true in more than 95 per cent of instances: church leaders are very busy, youth leaders are disorganised and last-minute, and young people don't like to commit to anything too early. If you remember those things when you're making your plans, you'll do just fine.

- Finally if you're going to be ordering more than 160 hoodies, don't forget to ask for everyone's hoodie size on the registration form!

If you're thinking about planning something similar, please get in touch. We'd love to hear about your plans and share what's worked well for us.

9

ConfiDANCE

Amy Boucher runs ConfiDANCE in Bristol. The project uses dance to help young people to explore life issues, talk about key topics and learn new skills. The project is faith-based, with Christian content ranging from 'being Jesus' to young people in dance workshops to Bible studies and faith-based discussions.

A passion for dance

ConfiDANCE started in 2010, following my experiences as a student youth worker in Bristol. I did a Bachelor of Theology degree through South West Youth Ministries (SWYM), with a practical placement at St Chad's Church in Patchway, South Gloucestershire. As part of this placement, I ran a free dance club called STOMP (Shout Truth Out—Movement Praise), which enabled young people to participate in fun exercise while learning about God through messages in music and discussions.

I found that dance improved the young people's attitude, engagement, self-esteem and achievement. It turned out to be a great tool for exploring faith and provided a safe place for young people going through tough situations, allowing them to explore what life is, share their thoughts and feelings and ask for advice on what the Bible says about their issues. I knew God was leading me to take this club to the next level, and so I created ConfiDANCE.

Dance has always been one of my main passions and interests. Growing up in Bristol, I had great experiences attending and competing with dance schools from a young age. Although I was grateful for the opportunities provided, I was aware that other young people were unable to afford this training, so one of my core values for ConfiDANCE was to provide *free* dance activities for young people.

The basics of ConfiDANCE

ConfiDANCE works on a not-for-profit basis and includes several dance streams to cater for different needs. As well as the original STOMP dance clubs, there are ConfiDANCE workshops, 'Family Fun' workshops (for young children and families) and Dance Fever camps—annual residentials organised in partnership with SWYM.

Finally, ConfiDANCE produces annual community dance shows called Dance Explosion. These are for all children and young people who have learned any dance routine through ConfiDANCE, and an invitation to perform is extended to other dance groups in the local area.

Our mission statement is 'To provide a dance ministry that is open and available to all young people, regardless of age, ability, culture and background'.

Although ConfiDANCE is made up of many different streams, all the elements are fun, increase confidence and self-esteem, encourage community involvement and are presented with a Christian ethos. This ethos is expressed through church involvement, exploring Bible stories, a particular song choice or simply putting Christian morals and ethics at the heart of the activities.

As I've mentioned before, it is really important to me that the activities are provided at no cost to young people. Many of the youngsters come from families who struggle financially to provide extra-curricular activities. Fees are covered by schools, churches, clubs or local authority community teams, and we often obtain grants.

ConfiDANCE ministry strands

The vision for ConfiDANCE is 'Dance-Dream-Achieve'. This vision works itself out in different ways throughout each stream.

STOMP dance clubs

With STOMP, we partner with local churches to run weekly sessions in their venue with a team of local volunteers. Through the clubs, we aim to teach and enhance the relevant skills of dance, to see how dance can be an appropriate, alternative form of worship and to provide skills that can be used in the future.

The activities in STOMP help young people go some way to realising their full potential, teaching them to dream big with God and giving them hopes and aims for the future using the skills learned through dance. We focus on exploring issues such as teamwork, leadership, diversity, self-esteem and confidence. At the same time, the clubs help young people to see God as part of today's culture, experience God for themselves and build community links to show God's love through performances.

Each STOMP session runs for one hour and includes a warm-up and cool-down, a dance lesson and a message slot and discussion. The sessions are tailored to accommodate different age groups, currently catering for children as young as three, with the oldest groups being for 16- and 17-year-olds. Dance styles range from hip-hop and freestyle to contemporary, lyrical and rock 'n' roll. Songs are chosen that are worship-based or that contain a message relating to God. During the break, there is a short talk, challenge or message to the dancers, with time for discussion.

To mark the end of learning a whole routine, STOMP dancers are invited to a church service or other relevant church event for a small performance, where they can invite their friends and family, as well as perform for church members in the local community.

ConfiDANCE workshops

ConfiDANCE workshops are school-based and aim to enhance many elements of the National Curriculum. Some workshops are developed to fit with PE or PSHE, while others are linked to the RE syllabus.

Like STOMP, the PE and PSHE workshops aim to teach relevant skills of dance and to provide skills that can be used in the future or for careers. The workshops cover teamwork, leadership, diversity, inclusion and supportive thinking and actions. We desperately want the young people to see an increase in self-esteem, self-worth and confidence to succeed.

Workshops for the RE syllabus have the same aims as PE and PSHE, but they also seek to introduce the idea that Christians use their talents in many ways and that dance is a relevant alternative form of worship. They explore the idea that, for Christians, God can be experienced and worshipped through dance, and he can help them achieve their full potential.

These workshops take place during lunch breaks or as after-school clubs or sessions within existing community youth and children's clubs. A variety of dance styles is used. The songs always contain a positive message, and, if it's an RE workshop, introduce a topic of faith.

In each session, the short talks and challenges address the positive message of the song, self-esteem and confidence, achievement, exploring the talents we have been given or using those talents to help others. Regardless of the stream chosen, all workshops are delivered with Christian morals and ethics at the heart.

To end the ConfiDANCE workshop or series, an opportunity to perform is given by the school or group, which could range from performing at the end of the day to a few classmates and staff to entering their group into a school talent show or dancing as part of an assembly or family open day.

Family Fun workshops

Family Fun workshops can be one-off special events or weekly activities in Early Years settings, schools or various private and local authority organisations. The workshops are tailored to younger children and their families, creating an environment where the whole family can learn together. As well as teaching skills in dance and movement, they enhance physical and creative development, positional and descriptive language, kinaesthetic writing actions and self-confidence. They enable families to interact with each other through fun and positive activities while developing bonds between family members.

We want to help families realise their full potential and keep building and chasing their dreams and aspirations. We also want to give families hopes and aims for a secure future using the confidence and skills learned through dance. Children are given the chance, through imaginative role-play in lyrical dance (for example, dancing a story), to see that they can be what they want to be and achieve what they want to do—now and in the future, with their family as a support. Parents are able to see increased value in their children and have a positive outlook for what they as a family can accomplish together.

We support the family in achieving new skills and sharing creative ideas. We also help them learn important life skills such as healthy living, exercise, basic literacy and numeracy, inclusion of other cultures and positive communication.

All dances and activities are created around a specific

theme. So far, we have developed the themes of healthy eating, an active lifestyle, communication, cultural traditions and storytelling. Family Fun workshops have also provided a chance for me to explore the provision of other activities alongside dance, such as craft, games and cooking.

Dance Fever

Dance Fever is part of a programme called 'Activate Camps' run by SWYM. These camps are open to any young person, of any ability, with the aim of helping them to explore faith through activities such as dance, football, music, fashion or outdoor activities.

The camp is a Bristol-based weekend away, full of dance training, focusing mainly on street dance. There are also lots of fun and team challenges, a surprise treat, confidence workshops, faith-related talks with small group discussions and a performance open to friends and family at the end of the weekend. We also run workshops as a taster of this weekend, which allow young people in churches to sample what the camp has to offer and book in for the full event if they enjoyed it.

This is the only element of ConfiDANCE that young people have to pay to attend. We run fundraising sessions to help interested young people to pay their fee to attend the camp. The camp shares the same aims as the other ConfiDANCE ministry streams but, being an explicitly faith-based event, it also challenges the young people to dream big with God and experience God's love in action, both in their own lives and in the lives of others.

Dance Explosion

Dance Explosion is a local charity youth dance festival. It is open to all schools, churches and organisations in and around the Bristol area, even if they are not part of ConfiDANCE. The event is designed to allow young people of various ages and abilities to perform together for fun with an educational and charity fundraising purpose: there is no competition involved.

Dance Explosion started in 2008, with the aim of providing an opportunity for groups and schools in nearby areas to work together, learn more about each other and produce a show together for an audience of family and friends. It also raises money for a local good cause in the process. Dance Explosion celebrates the achievements of young people in the area and enables young people to feel supported in their talent, to grow in confidence and self-esteem through performing and working together and to develop community cohesion with all ages in the local area.

A widespread impact

Activities based on achievement, behaviour, confidence and aspirations through dance skills and performances were greatly needed, and ConfiDANCE has made a significant impact on the children and young people involved. I have seen their confidence grow through public shows, and their standards of achievement are rising every time.

There has always been a natural expansion in the size of each club. When new clubs start, they are filled by word of mouth: young people tell their friends, such is their enjoyment. The members also work hard to raise funds to buy props and costumes to use in their dances and to secure places on the Dance Fever camp.

Many dancers have developed an interest in exploring faith and asking questions, resulting in some young people attending church and discipleship programmes, and a few considering baptism. Some of the first young people involved in ConfiDANCE have been baptised and are now wholeheartedly following Christ. I had the privilege of baptising one of these girls, and she is now my godchild. I am so proud of every dancer and I can see how much God is working in them through their talents.

The dancers and the clubs they attend are all well supported by parents and families, and it has been great getting to know everyone involved. This support has grown mainly as a result of running classes for younger age groups. When I was just doing youth work, I didn't get to see the families very often, as the young people had enough freedom to attend by themselves. However, when the children are younger, whole families bring their child to sessions and performances, not just to watch the dancing but to hear the faith discussions for themselves. This offers a great opportunity to get to know parents as well as siblings, grandparents and extended family.

ConfiDANCE has been running just long enough for these younger children to have become teenagers, so I already know their families. While talking to parents, I have been told that they love to see their children dance and to notice their confidence levels rising at home and in school. They appreciate not having to pay for sessions, as some families have several children attending.

ConfiDANCE has also had an impact on the wider community through local volunteer helpers partnering with schools and churches and inviting the whole community to watch performances. Dance is a form of communication that can reach across all generations. It has helped to break stereotypes, helped traditional church members to see alternative forms of worship and shown that young people do not deserve a bad reputation, as many work hard to achieve good things. Similarly, it has helped children and young people to see that people of all ages are interested in what they do, and that there are relevant activities and a place for them within the church today. Finally, for the families involved, it has helped them to recognise that the church is interested in their family: activities are open and available to all who walk through the door.

Where next?

When I first started ConfiDANCE, I thought I would just be working with young people, running STOMP dance clubs within church settings, but very quickly it became clear that God was expanding the ministry into many sections of the community. Something that started in churches soon became of interest to schools, and then spread to nurseries, children's centres and private and council-run projects. In addition to expanding locations, the age range grew. There was a high demand to start dance clubs for children as young as three years old and to keep young people right up to the age of 18.

I believe that God's reason for expanding the ministry in this way was to develop a lifelong journey of faith with the individual dancers. Instead of having large numbers of young people starting ConfiDANCE with no Bible knowledge, many of the dancers have started getting to know Bible stories in the younger groups and are therefore able to engage much more fully in faith discussions and add to their knowledge as they get older. I can see that God is still expanding ConfiDANCE by adding more local sessions and different streams to cater for new needs that include the whole family, and expanding beyond Bristol through residentials and workshops.

I am currently looking at the fact that God is leading ConfiDANCE to be a long-standing ministry with a long-term commitment from the children and young people attending. I am just reaching the point where the first young people who joined ConfiDANCE are approaching their 18th birthday or the age when they are due to leave the school that holds the dance club. I know that God has a plan for these young people as they move on and approach adulthood, and I am starting to explore which possibilities God would like me to pursue. One of the options is for the young people to develop their leadership qualities by helping with younger groups—leading the warm-up and cool-down, assisting with choreography and sharing their experiences during discussion times. I would also like to use their other skills to enhance ConfiDANCE. For example, one of our 17-year-olds is at catering school, so he came as a young leader to Dance Fever to assist with the food preparation as well as dancing. He did a great job.

I also feel that God is leading these young people into relationships with one or two key people within the church community, so that they can experience church life beyond ConfiDANCE. For some of the youth, this will be a local youth worker at a partner church, who can invite them to age-appropriate discipleship groups. For others, it will be an older member of the congregation who has taken on a mentoring and pastoral role to help individuals integrate into church life. A couple of the young people have developed a love for leading and singing, and are now a part of their local church worship band. They also help to lead midweek children's groups.

However, the reality is that, for some young people, there is no other group for them and no one in a position to take on a mentoring role, which raises the challenge of bridging the gap between ConfiDANCE and local church communities, to help young people on their spiritual journey. This is the area in which I do not have answers yet, but I know that God moves when the time is right.

Running a dance ministry in your own context

- Be relational: I find it most important to value each young person by making the time just to chat and take an interest in other parts of their lives. Without this contact, they will simply learn a skill and leave, never developing a genuine relationship with leaders or other members.
- Be flexible: tailor-make the activities and discussions to the interests of your own group of young people. If they are not yet confident with your chosen activity, don't be disheartened. Focus on confidence and skills, building activities at a comfortable level for them, and they will naturally progress from there.
- Create opportunities: children and young people thrive when given opportunities to lead activities and showcase their newfound confidence and skills by demonstrating them to others.
- Be financially wise: in order to provide free dance sessions, I have had to become very familiar with a variety of grant funding organisations and how to write grant applications. When I am not teaching or planning dance sessions, I

am always communicating with churches, schools and companies to access different funding opportunities.

- Build a team: the support of a committee, group of reference or simply a team of people willing to pray for you is invaluable. The ConfiDANCE committee members help with accountability, pray for the project and have relevant skills and expertise to help with finance management, funding and development.
- Network: getting to know people from local churches, schools and youth organisations can lead to a great amount of help and support with prayer, volunteers, publicity, financial provision and potential hosts for your ministry.
- Step out: if you have a passion to set up a specific project, don't be afraid to take that leap of faith. Draw on any relevant training and experiences to develop the ministry and take up more training opportunities as the ministry progresses. I didn't know what was going to happen as I started ConfiDANCE, but I can honestly say that God has provided and opened doors at every step of the way.

10

Messy Church

Lucy Moore is the pioneer of Messy Church, a rapidly growing ministry that is now found in over 20 countries worldwide. She promotes Messy Church nationally and internationally through training and speaking events, and she also puts considerable effort into discerning the development of the movement. This includes catering for those who came to Messy Church as children and want to remain part of the community.

The next generation?

Most Messy Churches have been running for two, three or four years now. In my own church, where we developed the concept, we've been going for over ten years. Such longevity is encouraging, but, as a Messy Church grows and matures, it encounters different challenges. One of those is how to disciple children who have become too old for the activities that are part of any Messy Church session. Many over-11s who have grown up in Messy Church want to remain part of the community, but churches sometimes panic with young people, thinking they become a kind of special case as soon as they hit 13. The question of how to involve and disciple young people most effectively through Messy Church is one that we have been grappling with for some time.

Back in 2011, we had a day in London for young people who help with Messy Church. Jointly organised by Messy Church and the Methodist Youth Participation programme, different groups came together with their leaders to talk through some of the issues. We wanted to give young people a voice—to hear what they liked about Messy Church, why they still go and what they feel they might contribute. We also suggested a few ideas to get their feedback and gave them a snapshot of the bigger picture, so that they could get a better view of what they were part of.

It was a great day, on which a wide range of issues was discussed. The gist of the young people's response was, 'Why do you assume that all young people are the same?' Some told us, 'Yes, we love going on leadership teams and we want all the help we can get with that; and yes, we'll lead stuff and take the initiative and take over the celebration and we'll run craft tables—whatever you want us to do.' Others said,

'This is for little children and their families; it's nothing to do with young people. I would never invite my friends to come to it. It's all very well for a few people to help with it, but it's not for young people, so you need a youth church for young people.'

There were strong views in both directions. Some were adamant that different youth provision had to be made, so that teaching, community and culture could meet the specific needs of young people. Other young people said that if you have a youth church for young people, then you need a 20s church for people in their 20s, a 30s church for people in their 30s, and so on, and that isn't what church is about. It's about being together and being vulnerable and learning together.

I heard again and again afterwards, from many of the adult leaders, that the day had given their young people the vision to see themselves as leaders and ministers in their churches, rather than just drifting into Messy Church leadership because their mum helps out. A lot of them went home buzzing from that day, thinking, 'I am part of the leadership of my church. I am valued. What more can I do?'

What next?

An anxiety seems to be bubbling up through the Messy Church network that when children get to the age of 10, 11 and 12, they will leave. Many communities are not sure what they can do. Some want to get the young people on the leadership team, but is that the right approach? It's what has traditionally happened in church, where young people get to the top of Sunday school and become children's leaders. But if Messy Church is seeking to reinvent church, is it right to do what has always been done? Is there a more imaginative solution?

I know this is becoming a pressing issue, and it has occurred to me to ask, 'Why aren't I discussing it with the youth workers? Why aren't I talking to diocesan youth officers?' They are the experts in this field, and there is a huge opportunity with children who have grown up through Messy Church. They're at the stage where they want to keep coming because they get fed, because their friends are there, because they like doing the stuff (although they don't like being seen to enjoy it—it's really not cool). Some are leaders; some aren't. What do we do with them and what do they do with us? Messy Church shouts out that it's all-age, and we really need young people to be part of the community, so that younger children can look up to them and so that adults keep in touch with the younger generation. But is this the right thing to do? Or is there something in the more traditional model of age-specific ministry, creating a separate youth group so that they can engage with appropriate material for their age and spiritual development?

It is a genuine question, because we want to get it right. We don't want simply to do what churches have always done, and we don't want to stamp our foot and say, 'But we're all-age and we won't consider anything that's segregated,' because that's not very profitable either. There are some examples of Messy Churches actively engaging young people, such as one Messy Church in Derbyshire where the young people took over the gathered worship section of Messy Church. The vicar, the Revd Chris Rees, said, 'You take the books, do your own thing and lead the celebration. You're in charge of the story and the song and the prayer.' They did exactly that and grew enormously through taking on this part of the ministry. Meanwhile, in Kent, the Revd Julie Coleman decided to start Trashy Church, taking the principles and shape of Messy Church but giving it a robust twist. They take junk in from their village and they upcycle it during the craft time. They might mend bicycles, put prams back together again, fix scooters or decorate furniture. Then they give the repaired items to people in the village who need them. This is part of their mission.

Trashy Church

Julie Coleman describes her experience with Trashy Church:

I have held Trashy Church at Adisham Village Hall for the past six months. This pioneer project is aimed at young people and families who are marginalised from society or church, feel too old to attend Messy Church or are seeking to move on from Messy Church.

The core of Messy Church is the Christian message, crafts and eating together. Trashy Church has the same message, but the craft itself has become the mission. The three parishes of Adisham, Aylesham and Nonington have responded positively with items that can be recycled. During the sessions, the people choose someone in the communities who has a need. They then recycle the trash by turning it into something that can be reused.

I held the first Trashy Church in November, supported by different members from each parish. All volunteers received minimal training in behaviour management with disengaged young people. I explained in detail to the young people and families that we are Christians within the Church of England, that I am a curate and that there will always be a Christian theme within each session. For our first session, the theme was

Matthew the tax collector. We heard about Jesus eating with Matthew's friends and we ended the session by sharing supper together. Our last session involved talking about the heroes in the Bible.

Very few of the young people and families have had any experience of the gospel or church. We were asked, 'Why are you doing this?' and we responded by telling them of Matthew's journey with Jesus and about walking alongside each other.

To date they have made and given four bikes, a scooter, a Trashy Christmas food hamper and a wheelbarrow for people in their community. Through the process, people have heard of this mission in Christ and now ask for our help. Trashy Church is due to renovate a garden and supply a bike after a request from a grandmother.

Feedback from one mother: 'I couldn't believe it. My son came home to say he had been to church and hung out with some Christians; and he says he plans to return.'

Feedback from another mother: 'My son never joins anything. I can't believe he has joined you; he had a brilliant time. Thank you.' These mothers, along with other families, are active members of Trashy Church. The young people at Trashy Church volunteer at Messy Church and are now putting together a worship band with help from one of the fathers.

Both Messy and Trashy Church have formed good links with Adisham and Aylesham primary schools, as well as ecumenically with St Joseph's Catholic School in Aylesham. We have now established a Messy prayer chain to support Messy and Trashy Church as well as those in the wider diocese.

TAKEN FROM THE MESSY CHURCH WEBSITE: WWW.MESSYCHURCH.ORG.UK.

I sense that there's an answer out there, or a range of answers, and I'm hoping that youth workers will be able to say, 'Here's an opportunity: we've got all these young people full of gifts, skills and the values of Messy Church—friendships and relationships and food. That's what young people do well. Here's a workforce just desperate to use their gifts within ministry.'

'Transformers' is a leadership course from New Zealand for young leaders. It starts from the premise that it's too late when young people are 13 or 14; we need to communicate the vision for leadership and servanthood in the church when they are 10, 11 or 12. The course takes place on a camp where the leaders work with the young people, mentor them and try to bring out gifts of servanthood. It's not just about who can play the guitar the loudest; it's about why we serve in a church, and how we can be more like Jesus. That's a scheme I would love to bring over here and use with the church, particularly with reference to Messy Church.

God has given young people different gifts, and leadership is not all about being up-front. We mustn't forget about the servanthood aspect of being a disciple. As I mentioned, people feel nervous about assuming that the only way for young people to carry on in Messy Church is to get them on the leadership team. Certainly this is one way, possibly the main way, but I think it's much more likely to be about friendships (more than 'relationships') between the team and the young people and between the young people themselves. Teenagers are much more likely to come as a group than as individuals.

In addition, I feel there's something to explore about intentional mentoring, because one of the aspects of discipleship that I think we can develop quite fruitfully in Messy Church is non-formal learning—or apprenticeship-type learning. We could set up non-scary apprenticeships, not for running Messy Church but for the Christian faith, where Christians (not necessarily older Christians, just those further along in their journey) and young people meet together. I want to say that's going to be the way forward—mentoring, coaching, someone intentionally accompanying another person on their journey of faith—but I've not seen it happen yet and I don't know of any framework in which it can happen. Some organisations have been thinking a lot about mentoring lately, but there hasn't been a worked-out framework for it. It's costly, very costly, and Messy Church leaders are stretched in doing what they do, without adding extras on. It's going to be tricky to say, 'Oh, by the way, as well as the ten crafts and the meal and everything, you've got to spend another hour a week with the young people.' That's going to be a big ask.

The messier we get on our Messy journey, the more wary we all are about instant fixes and courses and programmes. Our catchphrase over the years has been, 'It's going to be messy!' I don't think there is going to be one solution, and we certainly couldn't claim: 'Here's a handy course—put your young people through this and they will pop out the other end as leaders or disciples or missionaries.' I think it's much harder than that; it's about friendships, and not just for young people but in all aspects of discipleship. Friendships are very costly, and I think that's going to be the problem for churches: there is a massive opportunity to work with young people, but the most effective way is not just to put on a course that will be over in six weeks. The question is: will you be friends with them? That means opening yourself up with them, being honourable, giving up time and committing to friendship: it's not something to be taken lightly. It's simple and immensely challenging. It's the long-term friendships that make a difference.

Involving young people in leadership: Dronfield Messy Church

Revd Chris Rees writes:

When I arrived at the church, the congregation were predominantly retired people. Our family was the only constant family there, so, as we made the move, we asked ourselves the question, 'How can we be an all-age church?' From the start, there was a cultural change in church, out of which the idea came to start a Messy Church.

A youth group was already established, but it had no real link with church. At the same time, the young people whose parents came to church didn't feel that they themselves had a place in church. So the youth group was not attached to Sunday church: it was primarily an outreach and an answer to the question 'Can we provide a safe place for young people with very low Christian input?' We were providing a space for youth rather than a place for any 'teaching'.

Two of our children went to the youth group and went to church as well, and there were some young people who joined Sunday church because it was all-age and they felt that they had no place in their own church. So we had a youth group generally not associated with church, and a Messy Church where probably 80 per cent of the people didn't go to the 'main' church, and most of those people didn't go to any other form of church.

It was out of that mix that the young people got involved in Messy Church. The first young person involved in the celebration team was our son—someone who had grown up in an all-age church congregation, not in Messy Church. He was given permission to have a go, and, if he made mistakes, there was a team of adults ready to help out.

His involvement drew in some of the other youth group members, and they too were included in different ways and at different times—not always in the celebration team, but certainly in running the event. A couple of older teenagers from non-church backgrounds were very active in putting together the crafts, happily sawing and hammering, so, within the Messy Church congregation, a youth element was involved in different ways.

These young people, however, had not grown up in Messy Church; they had come from the pre-existing youth group. We were less successful in involving the children who were growing too old for Messy Church, although those young people did start to take responsibility for part of the celebration, in a way that was quite impromptu. Instead of doing the activities suggested, they got together, looked at the Bible passages and themes and said, 'OK, what are we going to do with this in the celebration?' Sometimes they produced a drama; sometimes they made a different contribution, which meant that the adults running the celebration had to be a little bit flexible on the day. One of the older girls was not so interested in contributing to the celebration and decided instead to take on the role of clearing up after the activities. My understanding is that she is still going to Messy Church.

I think there is still a real challenge in working out how Messy Church can grow with the children who are growing in it, and a certain amount of creative thinking is needed. As part-time Messy Church adviser for the Derby Diocese, I've visited quite a number of Messy Churches, and the issue is that we've put Messy Church together in a format that is, to some extent, age-limiting. How do we look at the format to make changes?

A related challenge is that the people who run Messy Church tend to see it as being for children and families, rather than young people and families. They have less experience in working with people over 12. Sometimes, in this situation, it can be scary to ask how we can live with young people among us in a way that helps them and the community to grow. Where are the resources and the help?

For some of the young people, joining the planning team seems to work; certainly, in the Messy Churches I've visited, I've seen this happening. Young people appreciate the relationships formed, both with young people of their own age and with the adults on the team. These relationships strengthen the all-age aspect of the community and help in the young people's faith development.

Young people do like to have a role, but not all young people want to help with the craft, run the technical side of Messy Church or take on some other task. Alongside leadership, how do we create a sub-community within Messy Church (not a separate community) for young people? If we don't struggle with that question, Messy Church will always be seen as a solution for the under-12s rather than an all-age community.

Involving young people in Messy Church in your own context

Alison Thurlow runs a Messy Church in Yate, South Gloucestershire, with a number of young people helping out. She gives a few pointers to how you might include young people in a Messy Church community.

- Having a larger number of young people gives them a group identity. If you have just one or two young people helping out, they might give up after a while, but the support of peers and the idea that they are doing something worthwhile together helps young people to take ownership.
- Entrust young people with as much responsibility as you would give to adults. Young people need to know that you trust and value them. See your role in working with them as something like a safety net—to be there if it doesn't quite go right.
- Let young people do things their way. You don't need to give step-by-step instructions all the time. All young people are creative and are able to come up with great ways of leading, facilitating or helping out in sessions, and they will learn lots while doing so.
- Review the session with the young people afterwards. Help them to decide what went well and what might not have worked, then give them some suggestions on how they might change things next time.
- Make sure you have a relationship with young people beyond their roles as leaders or helpers. Find out how they're doing at school, who their friends are and what their likes and dislikes are. Value them as more than just workers in your team.
- Don't expect young people who have grown up in Messy Church to join the main congregation or Sunday youth groups. They may well do so, but, if Messy Church is an expression of church, then remaining in the Messy Church community is a valid option.

The way forward

Where now?

Here we are at the end of the book. You've discovered ten different ministries, each working in a specific context with specific aims. What should you do now? Start by asking yourself these questions:

Which ministry excited you most?

Each of the ministries that tell their story in this book is exciting, but there might well have been one or two that really got you thinking. This is the Holy Spirit giving you a nudge. Listen to the Spirit's prompting as you think and pray about possible future directions.

Carefully think through what it was that excited you about those ministries. Was it the young people they reached? Did you recognise that your context is similar to the one described? Identify the answers to those questions and use them as your base for moving forward.

What is your local context like?

What's happening in your local community? Is there a 'tribe' of young people being ignored by the people around them? Do you have a secondary school in your parish or local area? Get together with others in your church and decide what the biggest need is. Are you able to start addressing it?

Who else might join you on your journey?

Are there any other bodies (churches, charities or councils) with which you might partner? Partnering with others means that you can pool resources and experience and increase your reach. Together, you'll generate more diverse ideas, share the responsibility, increase credibility and create strong community links.

How do I start?

Go back to the chapters you'd like to look at more closely. Take note of how the ministry started in the context featured in the chapter. Look at the tips from the writers on how to get going with that particular ministry. Follow their advice and adapt it for your setting: remember, you're the one who knows your situation best, so use the tips as guidelines rather than step-by-step instructions.

How will you pay for it?

Money: it's not nice to think about, but you need to consider how you're going to fund the work. Can your church raise funds? Are there any grants that you could apply for? There is a range of grant-making bodies, both government and charity-based. Do some research and select the most appropriate option for you. If you need to fill in application forms, there may be people in your church community who can help you.

Will your church community support you?

This means more than just financial support. Will your community get behind you and support you with encouragement and prayer? Starting out with the backing of your church means that you won't be out on a limb as you work. Getting people's support doesn't mean that everyone has to be involved at every step and in every decision— rather, that the whole church has signed up to the ministry and has committed to the vision.

It is striking that, in all the stories in this book, relationships and long-term commitment play a central part. The ministries explored are so diverse (urban and rural, church-based and detached, across many different special interests), yet these two values remain at their core. People have found ways to reach out to a certain group of young people and have stuck at it, even when circumstances, the authorities, other Christians or the young people themselves have disappointed them. They have all emphasised the need for honest, authentic and appropriate relationships with the young people who are part of their ministry or community. Whatever you choose to explore, make sure that these values are integral to your plans.

Of course, too, each ministry stems from God. Each one yearns to tell young people about Jesus and help them in their journey of knowing him. Each one was steeped in prayer at its conception and continues to be at the centre of a web of prayer that extends far beyond those taking an active part in the day-to-day running of the ministry. Each one is the result of a continued reliance on God's guiding and provision. As we reflect on where we are and where we might go, we need to keep God at the centre. It seems like stating the obvious, but sometimes we need to reiterate what's right before our eyes.

So, as we come to the end of the book and you consider where God is leading you and your youth ministry, remember the advice we gave right at the start.

Be brave.

Work with others.

Be willing to fail.

Hold your ministry lightly.

And trust God.

Further reading

Jo Dolby and Richard Passmore, *Pioneer Youth Ministry* (Grove, 2013).

Kara E. Powell and Chap Clark, *Sticky Faith: Everyday ideas to build lasting faith in your kids* (Zondervan, 2011).

David Kinnaman and Gabe Lyons, *unChristian: What a new generation really thinks about Christianity* (Baker, 2012).

George Lings (ed.), *Messy Church Theology: Exploring the significance of Messy Church for the wider church* (Messy Church, 2013).

Gill Marchant and Andrew Smith, *Top Tips on Welcoming Children of Other Faiths* (SU, 2007).

Matt Wilson, *Concrete Faith* (Message Trust, 2012).

Tim Sudworth with Graham Cray and Chris Russell, *Mission-Shaped Youth: Rethinking young people and church* (Church House Publishing, 2007).

Roy Crowne and Bill Muir, *The Art of Connecting* (Authentic, 2003).

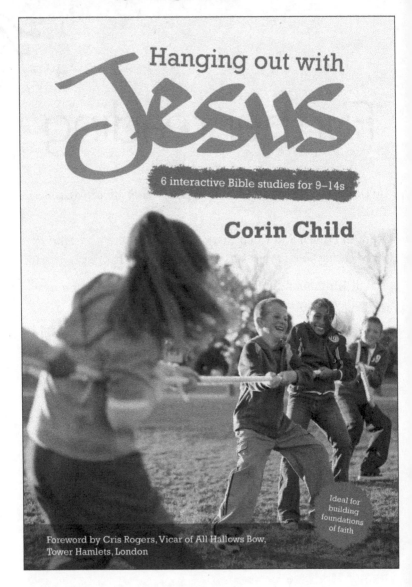

ISBN 978 1 84101 790 7   £8.99   48pp
Available from your local Christian bookshop or direct from BRF:
please visit www.brfonline.org.uk

cpas brf

GROWING
young leaders
A practical guide to mentoring teens

Ruth Hassall

Foreword by Dr John Sentamu,
Archbishop of York

ISBN 978 1 84101 637 5   £7.99   128pp
Available from your local Christian bookshop or direct from BRF:
please visit www.brfonline.org.uk

MAKING
DISCIPLES
IN MESSY CHURCH

Growing faith in an all-age community

Paul Moore

Foreword by Graham Cray

ISBN 978 0 85746 218 3   £6.99   128pp
Available from your local Christian bookshop or direct from BRF:
please visit www.brfonline.org.uk